WORLDWIDE SOURDOUGHS FROM YOUR BREAD MACHINE

Donna Rathmell German And Ed Wood

BRISTOL PUBLISHING ENTERPRISES, INC.
San Leandro, California

A NITTY GRITTY® COOKBOOK

Printed in the United States of America.

ISBN 1-55867-095-5

Cover design: Frank Paredes
Front cover photography: John Benson

CONTENTS

SOURDOUGHS AND BREAD MACHINES: A CONTROVERSY

When the first cookbook that addressed bread machine baking (*The Bread Machine Cookbook* by German) was published in 1991, there was an enormous pent-up demand for recipes and information for the machine that has set the bread world afire. Now, several years later, there is new demand from bread machine owners —this time for recipes and directions for a special category of breads, sourdoughs.

So Donna German, bread machine advocate, and Ed Wood, sourdough purist, joined forces to explore the possibilities of producing real sourdoughs in a machine. What they produced required give and take from each of them.

For Ed Wood, who has studied and collected wild yeasts from around the world for over 40 years, believes uncompromisingly in using only wild yeast, *with no addition of commercial yeast*, to produce sourdough flavors that cannot be produced in any other way. But because most of the bread machines in homes today have fixed, computer-driven timed cycles and stir-downs that may interfere with the requirements of sourdough cultures to produce these exquisitely flavored loaves, special techniques are required.

And Donna German, who has responded to thousands of bread machine users, believes that although there are many home bakers who will learn the special techniques and achieve the great rewards of working with only wild yeast, there are others who will find the varying reliability of making authentic sourdoughs somewhat frustrating.

Hence the bottom line: a book that challenges the bread machine baker to produce authentic sourdoughs using only wild yeast, with complete information about how to do that; and the addition of a "pushbutton" chapter which adds commercial yeast to recipes that are intended for the machine's full cycle, significantly reducing the sour flavor of the authentic breads, but nontheless producing sourdough breads more likely to succeed time and again.

All authentic sourdough full cycle recipes and most of the authentic dough cycle recipes (the dough cycle produces the most reliable results) were developed by Ed. The "pushbutton" chapter, with recipes that add commercial yeast, was developed solely by Donna.

Both of the authors agree that sourdough bread machine baking requires a special technique. There are literally hundreds of thousands of sourdough cultures in use around the world. Some have been passed down from generation to generation and are thousands of years old. Others are made today, in kitchens like yours. Each culture has its own personality and flavor, and may react differently from one day to the next.

One culture will work slightly differently in Donna's test kitchen in South Carolina than it will in Ed's kitchen in Idaho or for someone else in San Francisco. A culture will vary according to how frequently it is used. Sourdoughs are anything but consistent! They are truly unpredictable and undisciplined. To be successful with sourdough baking, it is necessary to develop an innate feeling for the activity level of the culture, the texture of the dough and the requirements to make the sourdough produce.

Sourdoughs in machines are a challenge —there is no precise equation. This book gives tools and hints, but success depends on experience, patience and experimentation. If at first you don't succeed, try try again!!

SOURDOUGH:
WHAT IS IT AND HOW DOES IT WORK?

Sourdough is a combination of one or more strains of wild yeast and various lactobacilli. Sourdough breads are *leavened* by wild yeast that produces a distinct texture associated with the "wild" bubble pattern in the dough. They are *flavored* by lactobacilli. These beneficial bacteria impart a unique sourness and exquisite flavor to sourdough.

Wild yeasts are everywhere in our environment — in the air, on plants, in flour — everywhere. They are so universal that some bakers collect their own by simply exposing a mixture of flour and water to the air for a day or so. They are not bacteria but are one-celled organisms called micro fungi and are much larger than bacteria. There are four major groups representing over 350 different species with countless varieties and strains.

With such an enormous number of wild yeasts, it should surprise no one that a yeast collected in Russia might perform differently than one collected in San Francisco or Saudi Arabia or anywhere else. We find, for example, that the Russian culture described in this book reaches its peak leavening activity in less than 2 hours, which is very fast for a sourdough, the norm being around 6 to 12 hours. This fast leavening makes it a perfect culture for use in bread machines.

Lactobacilli are just as diverse and numerous in the environment as are wild yeasts. The different species produce specific flavors not only in sourdough, but in cheese, yogurt, tofu and numerous natural products.

Sourdough cultures from different areas contain specific yeast and lactobacilli characteristics of those areas. For example, most of the bakeries in San Francisco use a sourdough culture with precisely the same wild yeast and lactobacilli. So striking is this combination that the lactobacilli has been classified as *Lactobacilli sanfrancisco*. The dominance of this culture is not because the bakeries have exchanged samples of their doughs, but is directly related to the overwhelming abundance of these organisms in the San Francisco environment.

Another characteristic of sourdough cultures is their amazing stability. From ancient times, bakers have recognized that they can preserve the same activity and flavor of a good sourdough by simply saving a small portion of dough to pass the organisms to the next batch of dough, to start the process over again —thus the term *sourdough starter*. The unchanging character of these starters, or cultures, is apparently due to the development of a symbiotic relationship between the yeast and lactobacilli. Each produces something essential to the survival of the other. In San Francisco sourdough the wild yeast spares the maltose found in flour which is essential to the lactobacilli. The lactobacilli, in turn, may produce an antibiotic which protects the culture from contamination by other bacteria and yeast.

It is the stability of sourdough cultures that convinced Ed Wood he might actually find one in Egypt that was the same combination of wild yeast and lactobacilli that leavened bread 5,000 years ago. New archaeological discoveries near the Giza pyramids have revealed an ancient bakery that apparently produced leavened bread at about 2500 BC. With the advent of current DNA technology it may indeed be possible to trace the origin of sourdoughs to their ancient ancestors.

The challenge to the sourdough baker is to produce the full flavor of the lactobacilli in a bread that rises exuberantly. And therein lies the crux of the problem. The lactobacilli plod along at their own speed. The average time for full flavor development approaches 12 hours. In the meantime the wild yeast, depending on which is used, is galloping along, multiplying like crazy, and may reach its leavening peak long before the lactobacilli have done their job. By the end of 12 hours the flavor is exquisite, but the yeast has exhausted its nutrients and become semi-dormant. The result is a good taste but poor leavening. All this can be readily resolved by waking up the yeast with another shot of flour 2 to 3 hours before making up the loaves, when the lactobacilli have just about completed their job. This bread will rise exuberantly and the taste will be out of this world.

Sounds complicated, doesn't it, when all you had in mind was dumping those makings in a machine and pressing the button? Well, it isn't that bad, but you have to know what's going on in a sourdough culture to really make it work for you, instead of against you. We'll tell you how.

SOURDOUGH CULTURES

As mentioned earlier, it is possible to collect your own sourdough culture by exposing a mixture of flour and water to the air for 2 to 3 days. Wild yeast and lactobacilli permeate our environment and will settle on the mixture and start to multiply. Unfortunately, a lot of other bacteria and molds will do the same thing and success is not assured. If you're lucky, the sourdough organisms may get a head start and create a slightly acidic medium that tends to inhibit growth of the undesirable organisms. If you live in a relatively or highly polluted area, your chances of getting a good sourdough free of contamination are probably diminished.

There are, however, a fair number of sourdough cultures on the market that have stood the test of time. Some of these do not contain commercial baker's yeast, but often the recipes associated with them do require it. *Once commercial yeast is added, the product is no longer a true or authentic sourdough.*

The cultures used to develop the authentic recipes of this book were collected over several years by Ed (see *Sources*, page 166). They came from the Middle East (the birthplace of bread), from Europe, Russia and North America. Most of them have been in use for hundreds of years and have been handed down through countless generations. They were developed during an era long before baker's yeast was invented and have never used commercial yeast in any form whatsoever. Goldrush Sourdough Starter (see *Sources*, page 166) was also used by Donna to test the authentic sourdough recipes; this wild yeast sourdough culture is guaranteed to contain *no commercial yeast,* and none was added to the authentic recipes during testing.

Bakeries have attempted to duplicate the sourdough process by using commercial baker's yeast for leavening and acetic acid for sourness. The results bear little resemblance to *authentic* sourdough. Unfortunately most traditional and bread machine recipes for sourdough have followed the same path. Commercial yeast has been selected, cloned, mutated, crossbred and interbred to produce a super yeast that blows uniform gaseous bubbles into bread dough at a prodigious rate. A packet of dried commercial yeast contains billions of organisms poised to eat everything in sight. If you use sourdough with baker's yeast, at best you destroy the exquisite bubble pattern and bread texture characteristic of the wild yeast. At the worst the tame yeast may overwhelm and destroy the wild one.

Never feed your sourdough culture anything but flour and water. There are a lot of sourdough substitutes —Hermans, Friendship Breads, Amish Breads, potato breads, etc. Most of them are nourished with sugar, milk and boiled potatoes or all three (or something else). All are characterized by a lack of stability and consistency and most need baker's yeast.

There is a substantial unfounded mythology on the behavior of sourdough cultures. Many authors caution against using metal utensils, citing the erosion of metal ions by the acidic culture. While we recommend plastic, ceramic or glass *storage* containers, stainless steel utensils will have no adverse effects and will outlast wooden utensils many times over.

Many sourdough bakers believe that their cultures require relatively frequent, perhaps weekly, feedings with flour to maintain their viability. The cultures used in these recipes are fed at 6-month intervals if not used more frequently. After long periods of refrigeration, cultures do become deeply dormant and may require several feedings at 12-hour intervals, after being warmed, to regain full activity. But they always do.

Although sourdoughs are acidic, they occasionally become contaminated by molds or strange bacteria which are probably introduced by flour. Such contamination usually becomes apparent after lengthy refrigeration when the sourdough organisms are dormant. The appearance of a culture jar can be exceedingly unappetizing. In spite of the visual and olfactory stimuli, these cultures can almost always be rescued by scraping off the offending growth, moving part of the culture to a clean jar, and then warming and feeding for several days.

USING YOUR SOURDOUGH

Your sourdough may be one that you inherited from your grandmother, collected in your backyard or purchased from a reliable source. Regardless of its origin, there are some things you must do to learn its inner secrets and some that you must never do.

To be successful with authentic sourdough, with or without a machine, you have to be committed to understanding a wild sourdough culture and know how to help it achieve its maximum performance. Remember that this is a living thing that may represent the progeny of a culture that started 5,000 years ago. In treating it with the respect and tender loving care (TLC) it deserves, you must *never* expose it to commercial baker's yeast.

To understand your sourdough, you must house it properly. You can put it in an earthen, ceramic or plastic jug and it will do just fine, but you can't tell what's going on. When you're activating the culture or determining its peak leavening activity, it's nice to look right inside. Ed says that nothing beats a 1-quart glass wide-mouth canning jar. It not only enhances that feeling of intimacy, but it is easy to clean and inexpensive to replace. Donna prefers to use a plastic container with a tight- fitting lid. The opening of the container is as wide as the container itself which makes it very easy to feed and stir the water and flour.

To really make a sourdough sing, it needs a warm environment after it comes out of the refrigerator. The ideal is 85° to 95°. It can be on top of your water heater, in an oven warmed by the pilot light, or in any other warm place. But always check the temperature with a thermometer.

The best solution is to fashion a "proofing box." Seek out an ordinary styrofoam cooler, the bigger the better. Throw away the top, turn it upside down and cut a hole in the middle of the bottom just big enough to admit a standard light socket. A 25-watt bulb should maintain the correct temperature. If you want to get fancy, put a light dimmer switch on the cord and you can regulate the temperature precisely. The box should be at least big enough to fit over your mixing bowls. It can also be placed over the top of your machine as a warming source during the mixing and proofing cycles if needed. Just be sure to remove it before the baking starts.

One final bit of intimacy. If you're using the culture every month or so, you don't have to feed it at all. If the relationship sours, so to speak, and you decide to break it off for a while, the question of maintenance comes up in case you patch things over and want to have another "wild fling." Store the culture in a refrigerator, and then warm it up and feed it about once every 6 months. The longer it lies dormant, the more TLC is needed to bring it back. Feeding every 12 hours for 3 to 4 days with vigorous stirring will always rescue it.

Now that you know everything you never wanted to know about wild yeast and sourdoughs, here's the bottom line. That jar of culture lying dormant in your refrigerator is the challenge to coax and manipulate it back to the force that has made man's bread since the dawn of civilization. Once you master that challenge, you'll make bread in your own kitchen that you can't buy anywhere.

ACTIVATING A DRY CULTURE

Most sourdough cultures on the market have been dried at a low temperature to preserve the viability of their yeast and lactobacilli. They must be "activated" before use by adding flour and water periodically until the culture forms a thick layer of foam on the upper surface. This activation may require anywhere from 24 hours to several days depending on the origin of the culture. As noted previously, the most essential ingredient of any sourdough bread is a fully activated sourdough at the peak of its leavening cycle. Activation is the first step in converting the dormant organisms of a dried culture to the active, metabolizing organisms of a wet one.

Place the dried culture in a 1-quart wide mouth canning jar with approximately ½ cup water at 95°-100°. Mix briefly and let stand 15 minutes. Then add ½ cup white flour, mix well and put in a warm place (85° to 95°). The lid should *not* be tightened. At this point the exact proportion of flour to water is unimportant. During the first 24 hours, swirl the culture occasionally. Depending on the origin of the culture, it may start to show signs of activity during this time manifested by a few bubbles on the surface. Regardless of activity level, at the end of 24 hours repeat the feeding process.

That is, add another 1/2 cup flour and 1/2 cup water and mix well.

Aggressive cultures will fully activate in 48 hours with 1/2-inch or more of bubbly foam on the surface. Less active cultures may require 3 to 6 days of repeat feedings every 24 hours. It is sometimes helpful to whip the cultures vigorously when mixing to add a little air to the mixture.

Obviously after feeding a culture in this manner for 3 days or so, your 1-quart jar will be running out of room. Simply transfer the excess to another jar and continue feeding them both.

It is important to observe a culture occasionally during the activation process. Fast cultures will reach their peak leavening in less than 3 hours and become semi-dormant by 12 hours. The bubble layer will flatten out and if not observed, the peak of leavening activity may be missed entirely, leading the observer to believe the culture has not activated, when quite the opposite has occurred. As the culture becomes active, it is wise to use caution when adding flour to a jar that is more than half full. Sourdough legends are full of stories about overflowing containers and the subsequent catastrophes.

Once activated, the culture can be used immediately or stored in the refrigerator. Neither dried nor activated cultures should be frozen. If refrigerated, it will again become semi-dormant. But in contrast to the dried culture, it will activate rapidly (3 to 9 hours) when removed, warmed and fed.

CULTURE PREPARATION

Culture preparation is the process of fermentation that takes place when the culture is warmed and fed with flour. It is continuous from refrigerator to the moment baking starts. During this time the wild yeast multiplies and produces the gases that make dough rise. The lactobacilli are also multiplying and making mild acids and alcohols that produce that special sourdough flavor.

Usually it takes the lactobacilli 10 to 12 hours to reach full activity, but the fast sourdoughs will have peaked and be semi-dormant by that time. One of the best schedules is to feed the culture with flour as soon as it comes from the refrigerator, mix it for 5 to 10 minutes in the machine, and then turn it off for 8 hours. At the end of that time, the remaining flour and other ingredients in the recipe are added and the machine is turned on. This gives the fast yeast a new supply of flour to reach its peak leavening during the last rise before baking. It also gives the lactobacilli sufficient time to produce their full flavor.

Although machine cycles differ substantially, the French bread cycle is usually the longest and has the longest last rise before baking. With slower cultures, it may be necessary to complete the recipe after 6 hours of proofing and schedule the machine to start 2 hours later, thus giving the slower culture more time to reach peak leavening.

Because of the rather tight timing requirements of baking machines, it is desirable to have some insight into the peak leavening interval of the culture being used (see

Table 1, page 16). So-called "aggressive" cultures metabolize flour rapidly, reach their peak leavening quickly and maintain that activity for a relatively short time (1-2 hours) before exhausting the nutrient supply. Slower cultures reach their peak in 9-12 hours but maintain that level of activity much longer (3-6 hours). For example, the Russian culture used in many of these recipes is very fast, reaching its leavening peak in about 1½ hours or less.

To determine if your culture is fast and aggressive or slow and laid back, remove it from refrigeration, feed it flour and water and warm it (85°-90°) for 5 to 6 hours. Fill a quart jar slightly less than half full with the warm culture, add ½ cup flour and ½ cup warm water, mix briefly and continue warming. An aggressive culture will produce a foam layer to the top of the jar in less than 3 hours. A slow culture will take 6 to 9 hours and may never produce more than 2 inches of foam. In either case when the foam layer reaches its top height, the peak leavening activity has started. When the foam layer begins to recede, the leavening interval is about over. The following table gives some information on approximate leavening times of some of the cultures used in testing the recipes in this book.

TABLE 1
LEAVENING TIMES OF SOURDOUGH INTERNATIONAL CULTURES

CULTURE	SPEED RATING	TIME TO PEAK LEAVENING	PEAK LEAVENING TIME	BREAD RISE TIME
Yukon	I	6 hrs.	4 hrs.	2-3 hrs.
San Francisco	I	6-8 hrs.	4-5 hrs.	2-3 hrs.
France	I	6-8 hrs.	4-5 hrs.	2-3 hrs.
Austria	S	9 hrs.	6 hrs.	3 hrs.
Red Sea	F	1½-2 hrs.	2-3 hrs.	1½-2 hrs.
Giza	S	9 hrs.	6 hrs.	3 hrs.
Bahrain	S	9-11 hrs.	6-7 hrs.	3 hrs.
Saudi Arabia	S	9 hrs.	6 hrs.	3 hrs.
Russia	F	1-1½ hrs.	2-3 hrs.	1-2 hrs.

S=Slow, I=Intermediate, F=Fast

NOTE: Goldrush culture has a fast speed rating and performs much as the Red Sea and Russia cultures.

FLOURS THAT WORK WELL WITH WILD YEAST

Other than the sourdough culture, the type of flour is probably the most important ingredient for success with sourdoughs. We specifically recommend bread flours over all purpose flours, since the former utilize a higher percentage of hard winter wheat. How high a percentage, however, is usually a complete mystery and various blends of less desirable wheats are probably present in most bread flours. The hard winter wheat contributes a better quality of gluten which is essential to bread baking. The amount of protein in a bread flour also offers a clue to the quality of the flour and is usually 13% to 14%. However, bread flours often contain additives to which some users object.

For the purist at heart, there is at least one partial recourse to the problem of what's in a flour: grind your own. There are a number of small efficient, relatively inexpensive home flour mills available. It is difficult, indeed, to beat the whole wheat flour that you produce by grinding Turkish Red hard winter wheat. And Turkish Red is easy to find (see *Sources*, page 166). Unfortunately the home mill doesn't produce a white bread flour. For that you may have to search out the smaller local or regional mills that are more service-oriented and tell you exactly what is in their bread flours.

Other flours include rye, whole wheat and two relatively ancient wheats, kamut and spelt. which have entered the market in recent years. Both kamut and spelt produce sensational sourdough breads.

KAMUT

Some 8,000 to 10,000 years ago, the wild grasses of the Middle East, through a process of natural cross-pollination, began to evolve into the early forms of wheat. Among the earliest of these were emmer, durum and kamut. Emmer is a grain with a tough hull that is exceedingly difficult to remove and it has now completely disappeared from the world market. The durums and kamut, however, thresh free of their hulls. The durums are hard wheats that have undergone an intensive selection process by plant breeders and are now used primarily in the production of pastas. Of these three ancients, kamut alone has survived in a form relatively unchanged by plant breeders.

The modern story of kamut is shrouded in both charisma and question. In the 1940s a serviceman from Montana was stationed in Portugal, where he was given a mere handful of giant grains of wheat reportedly taken from King Tut's tomb in Egypt. These seeds were eventually planted on a farm in Montana and for the next 40 years kamut enjoyed or suffered the ups and downs of an unknown and unusual wheat. In 1986 the Montana Flour and Grain Company began the organic production of kamut and the success of King Tut's grain has been on the upswing ever since.

Interestingly, the whole story of the origin of kamut has come under scrutiny. Its survival in a viable state from King Tut's tomb appears highly questionable. The name kamut, which is an ancient Egyptian word for wheat, was coined by Bob Quinn of

Montana Flour and Grain. It is apparently no longer grown in Egypt and its original source is a matter of speculation. There is, however, no speculation about the unique qualities of Bob Quinn's kamut. This giant grain is two to three times the size of most modern wheats. It can be substituted for hard winter wheats, soft wheats and durum in many applications. And perhaps most astonishing, in a nutritional analysis of Quinn's 1988 crop, kamut had a protein content of 17.3%, which was 40% higher than the USDA average of all U.S. wheats at 12.3%.

Bob Quinn's organically grown Montana kamut has a rich, distinct, nutty flavor which is so perfectly balanced by the unique flavor of sourdough that the two are destined for a long relationship.

SPELT

The second ancient grain to appear on the scene, spelt, is also the product of naturally occurring cross-pollination between wild grasses and developing grains. Plant breeders believe that spelt was produced accidentally by such crosses about 2500 B.C., although others believe the grain originated over 9,000 years ago. It has been a major food source in Europe for thousands of years and is common in European natural food stores today. It was apparently first cultivated in this country by Amish farmers in Ohio, where it was used primarily as livestock feed. But in the late 1980s, Wilhelm Kosnopfl, entrepreneur and president of Purity Foods, provided funds to finance a spelt breeding program at Ohio State University. In 1989 he opened a new facility at Okemos, Michigan, to provide spelt products to the health food market.

Spelt is another grain which retains its tough outer husk and special processing equipment is required to dehusk it. The grain is grown organically and like kamut, has a significantly higher protein content than bread wheat — some 30% higher. It also has a distinct flavor and texture that blends perfectly with sourdoughs.

The marketing claims for kamut and spelt suggest both are hypoallergenic and encourage those with wheat or gluten allergies to explore these two grains and their flours. The evidence at this time lacks well controlled clinical trails and those with wheat intolerance should consult their physicians or experiment with caution.

KEYS TO SUCCESS

HINTS
QUESTIONS AND ANSWERS

- Recipes are given in three different sizes, so that you can select the appropriate size for your machine.

- Warm liquids in the recipes. The liquid should be warm to the inside of your wrist.

- Never hesitate to experiment. Sourdoughs are tolerant to changing ingredients, kneading times, proofing times, etc. If the final result doesn't meet expectations, analyze the process, change it and see what happens.

- It cannot be overemphasized that the home baker does not always know the precise amount of flour and water in a sourdough culture. Equal parts of flour and water result in a mixture of intermediate thickness. As the percentage of flour increases, the mixture obviously becomes thicker. Table 2 on page 22 shows that 2 cups of culture of medium thickness contains approximately 1⅓ cups each of flour and water. If the culture is somewhat thin, it will contain more than $1\frac{1}{3}$ cup of water and exceed the maximum fluid allowance of most recipes in most machines — the moist dough will fall during baking. You must watch carefully in case you need to add more flour during mixing.

- The more often a culture is used, the more rapidly it reaches its peak leavening activity (within limits). And conversely, if the culture has been refrigerated longer than usual, it will take longer to peak. The time to reach peak leavening is of crucial interest to the machine baker who wants to start the machine at the right moment to utilize that leavening activity.

- A special note about sourdough. When it dries, it develops the texture and structure of glazed tile. The moral: Clean it up as you go along when it's wet, soft and easy.

TABLE 2
CONVERSION TABLE

1 cup culture	=	$\frac{2}{3}$ cup water, $\frac{2}{3}$ cup flour
$1\frac{1}{2}$ cups culture	=	1 cup water, 1 cup culture
2 cups culture	=	$1\frac{1}{3}$ cups water, $1\frac{1}{3}$ cups flour
3 cups culture	=	2 cups water, 2 cups flour

FREQUENTLY ASKED QUESTIONS

How do I activate a dry culture?

1. Place the dry culture in a 1-quart, wide-mouth jar or a similar sized plastic container with a tight fitting lid.
2. Warm ½ cup of water to 95° to 100° and add to the culture. Mix briefly and let it rest for about 15 minutes.
3. Add ½ cup bread flour, and mix all ingredients briefly.
4. Place lid on jar but do not tighten. At this point, the consistency is not important.
5. Place jar in a proofing box (made of styrofoam with a 25-watt bulb, see page 11). Any similar warm (85° to 90°), draft-free location may be used. It is essential to check the temperature of your warm spot with an inexpensive thermometer.
6. Repeat steps 2 through 5 every 24 hours until foamy bubbles appear on top which indicate that the culture has become fully activated. This process may take anywhere from 3 to 6 days. Fast cultures (Russian or Red Sea) are usually ready in 48 hours.
7. If you run out of room in the quart jar during the activation process, simply divide the culture between 2 or 3 jars and feed each one. Each may be used in subsequent baking.

8. The culture is fully activated when there are several inches of foamy bubbles on top and throughout the culture. Once the culture has become fully activated, use a portion immediately or store the entire amount of culture in the refrigerator.

How long will it take to activate it?

It may take up to 2 days for a fast culture or up to several days (3 to 6) of feeding a slow culture until it is foamy and bubbly. Don't rush the process by trying to use the culture if it is not ready, as your loaves will not rise.

It is desirable to check the activity every 2 or 3 hours. For example, if you don't check it for 12 hours, it may pass its peak activity and become semi-dormant (flat), leading you to believe that it has not activated.

How will I know when the culture is ready to use?

The culture will form a layer of foam or bubbles on top, sometimes rising all the way to the lid of the jar. Sourdoughs have been known to overflow their jars, so make sure you start the feeding process with your jar less than 1/2 full.

What is the consistency of the culture when it is ready to use?

The culture will be about the consistency of a thick pancake batter. If you are baking on a daily basis, it may be relatively thick and ropy with clumps or clots.

How do I use the authentic culture once I know it is ready?

1. If the culture has been refrigerated, it may be used straight from the refrigerator without requiring any warming — the machine will do that. If the culture has just been fed and you see your first layer of foamy bubbles, it may be stirred and used immediately.
2. Measure out the amount of culture required for the recipe and place it in the machine with half of the white bread flour.
3. Turn on machine and mix the culture and flour for 5 minutes.
4. Turn off the machine after the 5 minutes. Let the machine sit idle for 8 hours. This allows the sourdough flavor to fully develop in flavor.
5. After the 8 hours have passed, add all remaining ingredients called for in the recipe.
6. Select the longest cycle on your machine. This will be either the French, sweet, whole grain or basic white cycle. In general, do not use the rapid or turbo cycles unless using a very fast culture every day. Start the machine.
7. Allow the machine to knead all ingredients together for approximately 5 minutes, and then check the consistency of the dough. If the dough balls up on the paddle and does not touch the sides of the pan while kneading, it is too dry. Add

water 1 tbs. at a time until the dough just begins to stick to the sides and bottom of the container. This is slightly more moist than a nonsourdough bread. If the dough does not form a distinct ball, it needs more flour. Add it 1 tbs. at a time until the dough just begins to stick to the sides and bottom of the container, forming a ball. This step is extremely important.

8. Allow the machine to do all the rest of the work. Remove the bread upon completion of baking.

What do I do with the remaining culture in the jar?

1. After you have removed the amount of culture called for in the recipe, you should have less than $\frac{1}{2}$ jar of culture remaining. If you have more than $\frac{1}{2}$ jar, divide your culture into 2 jars.
2. Feed the culture with 1 cup of warm (95° to 100°) water and 1 cup of white bread flour. Mix all ingredients briefly.
3. Place lid on jar but do not tighten completely.
4. Place jar in a proofing box (made of styrofoam with a 25-watt bulb, see page 11) or similar warm place for 45 to 60 minutes (no longer) and then place jar in the refrigerator until the next use.

What do I do if loaves are not rising?

If the culture has not been used in a month or so, it may require 1 or 2 feedings prior to using to bring it back up to its fast rising capacity. The more often the culture is used, the faster it is, and the better it will rise.

1. Remove the culture from the refrigerator.
2. Divide the culture in half, placing each half in its own 1-quart wide-mouth jar or plastic container.
3. Add ½ cup warm (95° to 100°) water and ½ cup white bread flour to the each of the cultures.
4. Place lid on jars but do not fasten tightly.
5. Place jars in proofing box at 85°. Leave jars in proofing box until foamy bubbles appear. There should be between ½ to several inches of foamy bubbles when culture has been fully reactivated.
6. Repeat feeding process every 12 hours (as above) until the foamy bubbles appear. This may take a few hours or from one to several days depending on how long the culture was dormant.

If you want to make the bread and do not have time to feed the starter, it is still possible to make a loaf:

1. Make the bread as described in steps 1-4 on page 25.

2. After 8 hours, add all ingredients called for in the recipe and turn on the machine for 5 minutes of kneading.
3. Check the consistency of the dough as described.
4. Once the consistency has been corrected (if required), turn off the machine.
5. Set the timer on the machine to start in 2 hours. This extra time will give the slower sourdough culture more time to rise.

Can I test my starter to see if it is ready to use?

Once the culture has been fed with some of the flour from the recipe, it takes about 10 to 12 hours for the *lactobacilli* (which provides the flavoring) to develop to its fullest potential. The wild yeast, however, may fully activate in as little as 2 hours or as long as 12 hours. It is necessary to time both the wild yeast and the lactobacilli to peak at the same time. It is for this reason that the culture is fed with only part of the flour initially — it both feeds the yeast and activates the lactobacilli. The yeast will peak in a certain number of hours but the lactobacilli keeps right on developing in flavor. The remaining ingredients are added to the machine a certain number of hours after the first feeding, so that the second peak of leavening from the remaining flour will occur at the same time the flavoring is at its height.

In order to estimate when the remaining ingredients should be added, it is necessary to know how long it takes your particular culture to reach its full activation or leavening power.

1. Remove culture from refrigerator.
2. Feed the culture with ½ cup of warm (95° to 100°) water and ½ cup bread flour.
3. Replace lid but do not seal tightly.
4. Place the jar in the proofing box (85°) for 5 to 6 hours.
5. Remove jar and divide contents into 2 jars. The second jar should be identified in some way and then filled to slightly less than ½ full.
6. Feed both jars with ½ cup of warm (95° to 100°) water and ½ cup bread flour and return both jars to the proofing box.
7. Return the first jar to the refrigerator after 45 to 60 minutes.
8. Check the status of the second jar hourly.
9. The second jar (the one which was just shy of half full) will start to form a foamy layer of bubbles.

How do I know if I have a fast or a slow sourdough culture?

If the foam reaches *the top of the jar in less than 3 hours*, you have a *fast* or *aggressive* culture which works well in bread machines. The suggested idle time for aggressive cultures is 8 hours.

If the foam reaches *2 or more inches in less than 6 hours*, you have an *intermediate* culture which may work in a bread machines but could be tricky. The suggested idle time for intermediate cultures is 6 hours instead of the normal 8 hours used throughout this book.

If the foam **does not reach 2 inches in at least 9 hours**, you have a **slow** culture which works well on the dough cycle, after which it is then allowed to rise for as long as necessary outside the machine.

I have a sourdough culture which has been passed down through my family, but I have always added yeast to recipes I make with it. I want to make an authentic sourdough without yeast. May I use it?

There are literally hundreds of thousands of different cultures available which have been passed down through families, which may be made at home or which may be available for sale. Because there are so many, it is impossible to test all starters for any book. The best advice is to test the starter as described in the previous question to determine whether your starter is fast enough for baking in the machine without using yeast as a leavener. Testing for this book was done using Russia sourdough culture and Goldrush, both fast cultures (see page 16). Remember, you must never use baker's yeast if you want an *authentic* sourdough.

Is the 8-hour idle time based specifically on a fast culture such as the Russian? If so, how much time would I let the machine sit idle for intermediate or slow cultures?

Fast cultures such as the Russian or Red Sea cultures are timed for the 8-hour idle time. Intermediate cultures such as Yukon or San Francisco starter should have an idle time of 6 hours; at which time all remaining ingredients are added to the machine, mixed for 5 minutes and the consistency adjusted as usual. (See Table 1, page 16, for information about leavening time for sourdough cultures.) At that point, the machine is turned off, everything sits in the machine for 2 hours, and the machine is then started over again. If you have a timer on your machine, it may be set to start the machine 2 hours later. See your owner's manual to determine how to set the timer on your particular machine. In general, if your machine cycle is 4 hours and 10 minutes, you would want to set your timer for 6 hours and 10 minutes. If your machine is set by dictating the time the bread will be done, take the actual time of the entire cycle and add the 2 hours to it. Add that figure to the current time. To determine whether your culture is fast or intermediate, see the question on page 29.

Is it really necessary to wait the 8 hours? Can't I just put all the ingredients in the machine together and start it?

It is true that your bread would probably rise with a fast culture, at least moderately well. The 8-hour wait is to develop the full sourdough flavor (caused by the lactobacilli) of the culture. The lactobacilli need approximately 10 hours to fully develop their flavor. The 8 hours is combined with at least 2 more hours of machine cycle time so that the flavor should be at its peak when the bread begins to bake.

What cycle should I use on the bread machine?

You want a cycle with at least 60 to 75 minutes of second rising time for most breads. This is available on all machines on the market at this time. Heavy grained breads may require even longer rising times. Recipes were tested on the machines using the cycles listed in pages 34-42. Authentic sourdough baking is complex and should be watched carefully.

Rule of thumb: The faster the starter the shorter the cycle may be. The slower the culture, the longer the cycle should be. Let's assume that you use a fast culture and that you make sourdough bread every day so your culture is very fast and aggressive. You may find that using a rapid/quick or turbo cycle will work for you. If, on the other hand, you make sourdough breads once a week or once in awhile, you will want to use a longer cycle in order to give the bread a longer rising time. Experimentation is necessary.

If your bread is rising all the way to the top of the baking pan prior to the start of baking and it then collapses, you should use a shorter cycle. Similarly, if your bread is not rising all the way, you may wish to use a longer cycle (if available). If your breads are only rising to half the size of the loaf pan, see page 27. Once you become familiar with your culture in your environment, it's easy.

How can I make my own sourdough culture?

Although it is easy to make your own wild yeast culture, it may not have high enough activity and aggressiveness for authentic sourdoughs. To make a sourdough culture that contains commercial yeast (for use with the "Pushbutton" recipes), follow these instructions:

Mix together in a large bowl or plastic container (preferably with a lid) 2 cups lukewarm milk or water, 2 cups bread flour and 2 tsp. dry active (commercial) yeast. Cover this mixture and place it in a warm, draft-free location for 4 to 7 days, gently stirring it once a day. You may notice that the mixture bubbles and may even collapse. This is an indication that you have a healthy fermenting process going on and it is ready to be used.

Take out whatever portion your recipe calls for, leaving at least ¾ cup, and put into the machine as directed. After removing the portion from the culture, the starter must be fed with equal amounts of flour and water as it is removed. A sour smelling liquid may form on top of the cultures which may simply be stirred back in.

BREAD MACHINES
AND AUTHENTIC SOURDOUGHS

Home baking machines fall into two broad types: nonprogrammable and programmable.

NONPROGRAMMABLE MACHINES

You must use very fast sourdough cultures to match the relatively short rising cycles of most nonprogrammable machines. To determine if your culture is fast or aggressive enough, see page 29.

Black and Decker machines are essentially the same as the *Zojirushi N-15* (see page 40 and 41).

Breadman machines are manufactured by *Seiko* (see *Seiko 215*, page 38). They have renamed the French setting the "European" and have added a beep to add raisins.

DAK machines are made by Funai Electric Co. based in Osaka, Japan. There are four different models which have been sold, with the later ones called "Turbo" because they have a turbo or fast cycle. The white bread cycle has a 60- to 75-minute last rising depending on which model you have. If breads are rising well, the turbo cycle may be used. The final rising is the same as the basic white, but the first rising is shorter. The entire basic white cycle takes approximately 4 hours. If breads are not rising, add the 4 hours to the current time and another 1 or 2 hours to set the timer.

Hitachi has four different models, the *101, 201, 301* and *102*. The *101* and *201* are essentially the same 1½ lb. bread cycles, but the *201* has jam and rice features in addition to the bread. The *301* has the same functioning bread cycles as the *101* except that the machine makes a full 2 lb. loaf. The *102* is the new (1993) model which has some slight changes in the interior of the machine, but everything else is virtually the same as the *101*. The bread setting has a final rise of 70 minutes versus a final rise of 45 minutes on the bread rapid setting. Start with the bread setting. If the bread rises excessively, use the bread rapid cycle the next time. If the bread has difficulty rising, add all ingredients after the initial 8-hour proof, knead for 5 minutes, turn off the machine and set the timer for 5:10 or 5:40 (a 1- or 1½-hour timer).

Maxim machines are a very early model made by *Seiko* (see *Seiko 12,* page 38).

National/Panasonic machines are made by Matsushita and are virtually identical except for the name. The 1 lb. machines are generally referred to as "55" and have one main kneading cycle following a preheating cycle. The 1½ lb. machines are referred to as "65" and have two kneading cycles — one initially before yeast drops in, the warming rest when raisins are added and the yeast drops in, and then the second full knead. The last rise after shaping is the same on all cycles and varies between 50 and 60 minutes depending on the computer sensors. The whole wheat cycles have longer risings before the shaping, so would be best for breads which are not rising well. Use the basic or rapid cycles if breads are rising well. They introduced a new multigrain machine in the fall of 1993 which has an even longer second rising than the whole wheat. While it was not available for testing for this book, the multigrain cycle may provide longer leavening for sourdoughs even though it still has only 50 minutes rising after the shaping.

Regal *Kitchen Pro, K6775* (1½ lb.) is the same as *Seiko 215* (see page 38).
    K6776 is the new machine introduced in the fall of 1993. This has normal and sweet settings with the difference being the baking temperature and not the risings. Both have a final rising of 60 minutes after the last shaping. Use the sweet cycle for

Both have a final rising of 60 minutes after the last shaping. Use the sweet cycle for sourdoughs which contain more than 2 tbs. of sugar or dried fruits or nuts. If the bread rises excessively, use the speed cycle the next time. If the bread has difficulty rising, add all ingredients after the initial 8-hour proof, knead for 5 minutes, turn off the machine and set the timer for 4:40 to 5:10 (large) or 4:30 to 5:00 (regular) (a 1- or 1½-hour timer).

K6773 (1½ lb.) has a French/whole grain cycle with a 75-minute final rise, perfect for most sourdoughs.

K6772 (1 lb.). The basic bread cycle (55 minutes last rise) should be used unless adding dried fruits, in which case use the raisin bread setting. If the bread has difficulty rising, add all ingredients after the initial 8-hour proof, knead for 5 minutes, turn off the machine and set the timer for 4:40 to 5:10 (a 1- or 1½-hour timer). If the bread still does not rise, you can increase the timer amount or remove the bread from the dough cycle and rise and bake conventionally.

K6771 is the same machine as the *Hitachi 101* (see page 35).

Sanyo *15* (1½ lb.) and *20* (2 lb.) are just being introduced in the fall of 1993 or winter of 1994. The *15* will have a 65-minute last rise on both the French and the basic bread cycle. The *20* will have a 54-minute last rise on both cycles. The second rising is longer on the French cycle than the basic so start testing with the French cycle. If the bread rises and collapses, switch to the basic cycle.

SMB12 has whole wheat, sweet and French settings, all of which are good for sourdoughs. The sweet setting actually has the longest final rise (75 minutes) and has a longer baking at a lower temperature. The basic cycle has a 65-minute last rise which is longer than the 45-minute last rise on the whole wheat cycle. Start with the sweet cycle. If the breads rise and then fall, switch to the basic cycle.

SBM11 has just the basic cycle with a 65-minute final rise. If the bread has difficulty rising, add all ingredients after the initial 8-hour proof, knead for 5 minutes, turn off the machine and set the timer for 4:00 to 4:30 (a 1- or 1½-hour timer). If that does not help, use the dough cycle and allow the dough to rise and bake conventionally.

SBM10 is an old 1 lb. machine with a final rise of 65 minutes on the bread setting. Follow the procedures for *SBM11*.

Seiko manufactures many machines under different names — usually *Chefmate* or *Mister Loaf*. Seiko machines typically have only one kneading cycle.

The *HB515* (1 to 1½ lb.) and the *HB 520* (1½ to 2 lb.) are new machines, introduced in the fall of 1993. They have a French setting with a last rise of 90 minutes, which is great for sourdoughs. If breads rise and then collapse, use a shorter setting such as the basic or sweet (50 minutes last rise). If breads are not rising well, set the timer for 6:00 or 6:30 (1-or 1½-hour timer).

The *210* model (1 lb.) and the *215* (1½ lb.) have a French setting with a 75-minute final rise after stir-down. A long (65 minutes) baking cycle gives a crispy crust but the bread may actually be removed about 10 minutes before the end of the cycle if desired. If breads are not rising, use a 2- to 3-hour (5:40 to 6:40) timer after adding all ingredients. If you bake sourdoughs frequently and the dough is rising excessively, use the standard (medium) cycle with a 55-minute final rise.

211 has only a standard setting with a final rise of 55 minutes. If breads are not rising, use the timer as above or rise and bake conventionally.

12W is an old model. The last rise is 75 minutes on the French cycle and is recommended for sourdough. If breads are rising and collapsing, try using the standard cycle with 60 minutes last rise. The time-saver cycle has only 40 minutes last rise.

Singer *Bread N Dough* is the same as *Seiko 215* (see page 38).

Toastmaster has two identical models of machines, they just have different packaging (the *1151* comes with two mixes and a knife). This 1¼ lb. machine uses the basic bread cycle for sourdoughs with a 65-minute last rise. If the bread has difficulty rising, add all ingredients after the initial 8-hour proof, knead for 5 minutes, turn off the machine and set the timer for 4:40 to 5:10 (a 1- or 1½-hour timer). If breads are rising and collapsing, try using the rapid cycle with 45 minutes last rise.

New machines planned for 1994 will have a whole wheat cycle and should be used in the same manner.

Welbilt machines are made by Funai Electric Co. in Osaka, Japan. The *ABM 100* is virtually the same as the *DAK* (see page 35) without the turbo cycle and has a last rise of 75 minutes on the basic cycle. The *ABM 150R* is programmable, which works well with sourdoughs (see page 41). The 1 lb. Welbilt machines have a 55-minute last rise after rounding. If the bread has difficulty rising, add all ingredients after the initial 8-hour proof, knead for 5 minutes, turn off the machine and set the timer for 1½ or 2 hours (3:45 to 4:14). If that does not work, use the dough cycle and rise and bake conventionally.

West Bend *Bread and Dough Maker* has a French setting with a 65-minute last rise which is a good place to start. If breads are rising and then collapsing, use the whole wheat setting (57 minutes last rise) or the sweet setting (55 minutes). If breads are not rising, set the timer to 4:40 to 5:10 (a 1 or 1½ hour timer).

Zojirushi *BBC N-15*. Use the dry milk setting with a total of 130 to 160 minutes of rising time (40 to 60 minutes after the final stir-down). If the breads are not rising well, try setting the machine on a 6- or 6.5-hour timer. If you bake frequently and the bread is rising very well, you may find that the fresh milk cycle works well (45-60 minutes last rise with shorter first risings). The "raisin bread" on each cycle has a slightly lower baking temperature which may be used if the bread is too dark or crusty.

BBC S-15. If you do not wish to use the programmable cycle (see below), the French bread cycle works well with 110 minutes of last rising. If the dough is not rising, try using the programmable cycle. If the breads are rising nicely the basic white cycle will work well with a 70-minute last rise.

PROGRAMMABLE MACHINES

With a programmable machine you can do just about anything that an experienced sourdough baker does by hand. In contrast to the nonprogrammables that require a very fast culture to adequately leaven a loaf in a relatively short time, almost any culture, fast or slow, can do the job in a programmable machine.

The **Welbilt** *ABM-150 R*, for example, gives you the option of one or two kneading times (one is ideal for sourdough), up to 170 minutes of rising time if the second kneading is eliminated, and a variable baking time up to 60 minutes. A manual mixing cycle and a 12-hour timer provide almost unlimited flexibility.

Zojirushi *S-15* offers even more. The users can program every part of the cycle, creating their own cycle, and store it in the machine's memory. The "Rest," "Rise 1" and "Rise 2" can each be extended up to 2 hours. Nearly ideal for sourdoughs. The user also has the ability to start and end each part of the cycle as the condition of the dough warrants. For example, if you decide that the dough has risen enough, you can start the bake cycle instead of frantically puncturing the surface to keep it from running over the top.

1. Set the first kneading for 10-15 minutes.
2. Set the "rest" to 10-30 minutes.
3. Set the second kneading to 0-15 minutes.
4. Set the first rise to 0-20 minutes.
5. Set the second rise to 90 minutes.
6. Set the bake time to 55-60 minutes.
7. Set the cooling time to 15-30 minutes.

(Note: With the *Welbilt ABM-150R* only (3), (5) and (6) can be controlled. With the *Zojirushi* all of the settings can be changed as desired and the changes stored in the machine's memory.)

With the Russian or other fast cultures it may be necessary to shorten the rising cycle to prevent excessive leavening. This flexibility, however, permits the baker to use slower cultures with longer delays and rising times which also produce a more sour bread. Cultures with slower rising times include those from San Francisco, the Yukon, Bahrain and Saudi Arabia.

AUTHENTIC SOURDOUGHS
FULL CYCLE
NO COMMERCIAL YEAST

Home baking machines fall into two broad types: programmable and nonprogrammable. With the programmable machine the user has *some* choices in setting the cycles to determine how long certain steps take. As used here, the ability to select various options such as yeast bread, sweet bread, whole grain bread, etc., does *not* qualify as a "programmable" machine. The nonprogrammable machine "fixes" the various cycles. The user presses the start button and comes back when the instructions say the bread should be done. Both types, however, have a timer that allows the baker to mix the ingredients and then delay starting the machine for a variable period. The timer is actually designed to produce the finished bread at a time most convenient for the baker — for example, just before breakfast. But for sourdoughs, the timer serves an entirely different purpose not envisioned by the designer. It permits the baker to allow the sourdough culture to ferment until it has reached its peak activity and then start the machine. Without the timer, most nonprogrammable machines could not produce authentic sourdough. With the timer, most can.

The trick to making sourdoughs in bread machines is to alter the programmable models as much as possible to meet the needs of sourdoughs, and to alter the sourdoughs as much as possible to meet the needs of the nonprogrammable models. Both types can produce better sourdough breads than most commercial bakeries.

We hadn't baked many sourdoughs in machines before becoming aware of an intrinsic difference between machine loaves and our usual sourdoughs. The machine-baked breads are distinctly and pleasantly more moist. Apparently the pan and oven shape reduce the loss of fluid during the entire process. The result is an unexpected plus for the machine.

These recipes were tested with wild sourdough cultures from *Sourdoughs International* and *Cal Gar Goldrush Sourdough* (see page 166 for ordering information).

BASIC DIRECTIONS FOR AUTHENTIC SOURDOUGHS

1. Remove culture from refrigerator.
2. Measure and then mix culture and flour (listed first) in the machine for 10 minutes.
3. Feed remaining culture with 1 cup bread flour and 1 cup water (Note: If adding more than 1 cup flour and water, add it in equal amounts. Adjust consistency by adding more flour if necessary until it is similar to a thick pancake batter). Proof for 45 to 60 minutes and then return to refrigerator.
4. Turn off the machine for 8 hours. Then:
5. Add the remaining ingredients to complete the recipe and start the French

bread cycle (see pages 34-42 for your specific machine).

6. Adjust the "paddle consistency" by adding flour or water 1 tablespoon at a time.

Note: Because the consistency of the culture will vary, you do not know exactly how much flour is contained in 1½ cups of culture. If the dough balls up on the paddle and rotates without touching the sides, there is too much flour and the blade is not kneading efficiently. Add water until the dough just begins to stick to the sides and bottom of the container. If the dough doesn't form a distinct ball, it needs more flour. Wait 3 to 5 minutes before making these adjustments to allow the dough to assimilate the recipe ingredients.

GENERAL HINTS FOR AUTHENTIC SOURDOUGHS IN BREAD MACHINES

- One of the keys to success in a bread machine is a fully activated, fast culture.
- If the culture is not fully activated, remove from refrigerator, and feed with equal amounts of flour and water. Or, separate the culture into 2 containers, feed both, save one for a "backup" and give one to a friend. The starter should be warmed in the proofing box for about 8 hours and then used as normal. If the culture has been sitting in the refrigerator for a long time, try feeding it like this about every 8 to 12 hours for several days until you see lots of

bubbles, foam and activity.

- The initial mixing of culture and half the flour may be done in a mixing bowl and kept in the proofing box for the 8-hour delay. That helps to keep things warm and activated. You can even mix the culture and flour in the machine for 5 minutes and then place the machine pan in the proofing box. It depends on how big the proofing box is.

- Deionized water (bottled drinking water) may act differently than city water. If you are having difficulty getting breads to rise, try using bottled water to see if it helps.

- The consistency of sourdough is somewhat more moist than nonsourdough breads. The dough may even crawl up the sides of the pan.

- The container of culture should be warm to the touch after the 45 minutes of proofing after feeding. Too high a temperature for warming the culture may have adverse affects. Too low a temperature may slow the activity.

WORLD BREAD

This is a generic white bread baked and eaten around the world. After the 8-hour proof, a warm fast culture will leaven this bread in 60-75 minutes last rise. A warm slow culture will require at least 90 minutes and will be more successful in a programmable machine that offers 120 minutes. With a fast culture, you can bake this recipe on the white or standard bread cycle. With a slow culture, you should use the French bread cycle which has a longer last rise before baking.

	1 lb.	**1½ lb.**	**2 lb.**
sourdough culture	1⅛ cups	1½ cups	2¼ cups
white bread flour	1 cup	1⅓ cups	1¾ cups

Knead for 5 minutes, allow to sit for 8 hours, add following ingredients and start cycle.

	1 lb.	**1½ lb.**	**2 lb.**
milk, warm	3 tbs.	¼ cup	⅓ cup
salt	½ tsp.	¾ tsp.	1 tsp.
sugar	1½ tbs.	2 tbs.	3 tbs.
vegetable oil	1½ tsp.	2 tsp.	1 tbs.
white bread flour	1 cup	1⅓ cups	1¾ cups

TANYA'S PEASANT BLACK BREAD

This bread is on our list of twelve best. It requires a fast sourdough to successfully leaven the rather heavy dough in the average machine cycle. If you have a programmable machine, stretch out the last rise to 120 minutes. Don't omit the vital gluten with this one. The coriander and molasses combination complements the sourdough.

	1 lb.	**1½ lb.**	**2 lb.**
sourdough culture	1½ cups	2 cups	3 cups
white bread flour	1 cup	1½ cups	2 cups

Knead for 5 minutes, allow to sit for 8 hours, add following ingredients and start cycle.

dark molasses	1 tbs.	1⅓ tbs.	2 tbs.
milk, warm	¼ cup	⅓ cup	½ cup
sugar	1 tbs.	1½ tbs.	2 tbs.
ground coriander	¾ tsp.	1 tsp.	1½ tsp.
salt	½ tsp.	1 tsp.	1 tsp.
vital gluten	2 tsp.	1 tbs.	1½ tbs.
rye flour	¾ cup	1 cup	1½ cups
whole wheat flour	¾ cup	1 cup	1½ cups
milk or water as needed			

LIGHT SWEDISH LIMPA BREAD

The dictionary defines "limpa" as a rye bread made with molasses or brown sugar. The origin of the Swedish tag is less certain. In any event, this is an outstanding sourdough that rates high on our best sourdoughs list. Use the coarse side of your kitchen grater to take off the outer surface of the orange rind. The individual strips are often 1/4- to 1/2-inch long. The brown sugar and orange rind are essential. While this is a relatively light dough, it will rise significantly better with added vital gluten. A fast culture will leaven this bread very well, with a 90- to 120-minute last rise before baking. Slow cultures will do better with a dough cycle, shaping and allowing the dough a longer rising period.

	1 lb.	**1½ lb.**	**2 lb.**
sourdough culture	1⅛ cups	1½ cups	2 cups
white bread flour	¾ cup	1 cup	1½ cups

Knead for 5 minutes, allow to sit for 8 hours, add following ingredients and start cycle.

water	2 tbs.	3 tbs.	1/4 cup
vegetable oil	2 tsp.	1 tbs.	1 tbs.
orange rind	1/2 orange	1 orange	1 orange
or dried orange peel	1 tbs.	1 1/2 tbs.	2 tbs.
brown sugar	3 tbs.	1/4 cup	1/3 cup
salt	1/2 tsp.	1/2 tsp.	1 tsp.
vital gluten	1 tsp.	1 1/2 tsp.	2 tsp.
caraway seed	1 tsp.	1 tsp.	2 tsp.
fennel seed	1 1/2 tsp.	2 tsp.	1 tbs.
white bread flour	3/4 cup	1 cup	1 1/2 cups
rye flour	1/2 cup	2/3 cup	3/4 cup
water as needed			

KHOUBZ

This is traditionally made into a pita bread (see page 100). However, it is also delicious baked in your machine. Use a French bread or basic white cycle.

	1 lb.	1½ lb.	2 lb.
sourdough culture	1½ cups	2 cups	3 cups
white bread flour	1 cup	1⅓ cups	2 cups

Knead for 5 minutes, allow to sit for 8 hours, add following ingredients and start cycle.

	1 lb.	1½ lb.	2 lb.
salt	½ tsp.	1 tsp.	1 tsp.
sugar	2 tsp.	1 tbs.	1¼ tbs.
olive oil	2 tsp.	1 tbs.	1½ tbs.
cumin	½ tsp.	1 tsp.	1¼ tsp.
thyme	½ tsp.	1 tsp.	1¼ tsp.
chile pepper	½ tsp.	1 tsp.	1¼ tsp.
onion, diced	3 tbs.	¼ cup	⅓ cup
white bread flour	1 cup	1⅓ cups	2 cups
water as needed			

LIGHT EGYPTIAN KAMUT BREAD

Kamut is that ancient grain of questionable origin — maybe Egypt, maybe somewhere else — but ancient. And different. This bread is so unusual that it easily made our list of best twelve. Kamut is destined to become much better known in the world of baking and perhaps especially in sourdoughs. This rises well with a fast culture and no delay.

	1 lb.	**1¼ lb.**	**1½ lb.**
sourdough culture	1 cup	1½ cups	2 cups
white bread flour	½ cup	¾ cup	1 cup

Knead for 5 minutes, allow to sit for 8 hours, add following ingredients and start cycle.

salt	½ tsp.	½ tsp.	1 tsp.
vegetable oil	½ tbs.	2 tsp.	1 tbs.
caraway seeds	½ tbs.	2 tsp.	1 tbs.
vital gluten	1 tsp.	2 tsp.	2 tsp.
kamut flour	½ cup	¾ cup	1 cup
white bread flour	⅓ cup	½ cup	⅔ cup
water as needed			

LIGHT AUSTRIAN SPELT BREAD

Spelt is not as ancient as kamut, although some trace its origin back 9,000 years and cite several biblical references. It was prominent in early medieval Europe and is a major cereal grain on that continent today. It is being rapidly discovered by U.S. bakers. This bread easily made our best twelve list. Try it. If you use a slow culture, schedule a 1-hour delay before starting the French bread cycle. A fast starter needs no delay. This recipe uses white spelt (as opposed to the whole spelt).

	1 lb.	**1¼ lb.**	**1½ lb.**
sourdough culture	1 cup	1½ cups	2 cups
white bread flour	½ cup	¾ cup	1 cup

Knead for 5 minutes, allow to sit for 8 hours, add following ingredients and start cycle.

salt	½ tsp.	½ tsp.	1 tsp.
vegetable oil	½ tbs.	2 tsp.	1 tbs.
fennel seeds	½ tbs.	2 tsp.	1 tbs.
vital gluten	1 tsp.	1½ tsp.	2 tsp.
spelt flour, white	½ cup	¾ cup	1 cup
white bread flour	⅓ cup	½ cup	⅔ cup
water as needed			

YUKON HERB BREAD

In August of 1896, gold was discovered on a tiny creek of the Klondike River and in two years more than 40,000 people stampeded up the Yukon River. The association between prospectors and their sourdough was so strong that the term "sourdough" in time was used to describe the man, not his bread. Use the French bread cycle.

	1 lb.	**1½ lb.**	**2 lb.**
sourdough culture	1⅛ cups	1½ cups	2¼ cups
white bread flour	¾ cup	1¼ cups	1⅔ cups

Knead for 5 minutes, allow to sit for 8 hours, add following ingredients and start cycle.

butter	2 tsp.	1 tbs.	1 tbs.
milk, warm	⅓ cup	½ cup	⅔ cup
salt	½ tsp.	½ tsp.	1 tsp.
sugar	½ tbs.	2 tsp.	1 tbs.
thyme	½ tsp.	½ tsp.	1 tsp.
oregano	½ tsp.	½ tsp.	1 tsp.
basil	½ tsp.	½ tsp.	1 tsp.
white bread flour	1 cup	1¼ cups	2 cups
water as needed			

SAUDI DATE BREAD

Dates have been a major agricultural crop in Saudi Arabia for centuries. You can buy dates that are already chopped and save some time. We added the dates and nuts at the beginning of the second kneading. If your machine has only one main kneading, add them at the beginning with all the other ingredients. If your machine is subject to the doughy blues, cut the amount of dates and nuts in half, place aluminum foil over the glass dome without blocking the air vents and use the sweet cycle or basic white cycle. Ed uses twice the amount of dates and nuts shown in the recipe (in Idaho). Donna had some doughy blue loaves in South Carolina. Use the sweet or basic white cycle.

	1 lb.	1½ lb.	1¾ lb.
sourdough culture	1 cup	1½ cups	2 cups
white bread flour	¾ cup	1 cup	1½ cups

Knead for 5 minutes, allow to sit for 8 hours, add following ingredients and start cycle.

sugar	1 tbs.	1½ tbs.	2 tbs.
water	2 tbs.	3 tbs.	¼ cup
olive oil	1½ tsp.	2 tsp.	1 tbs.
salt	½ tsp.	½ tsp.	1 tsp.
dates, chopped	¼ cup	⅓ cup	½ cup
walnuts, chopped	¼ cup	⅓ cup	½ cup
bread flour	¾ cup	1¼ cups	1½ cups
water as needed			

INNSBRUCK LIMPA BREAD

This Austrian limpa is a sweeter, more highly seasoned and heavier dough than the Swedish limpa (page 50). It is one of the best rye recipes from Austria. This rises well with a fast culture. Add the raisins at the beginning or at the beep or appropriate time for your machine. Make this on the French bread cycle.

	1 lb.	**1½ lb.**	**2 lb.**
sourdough culture	1½ cups	2 cups	3 cups
white bread flour	½ cup	⅔ cup	1 cup

Knead for 5 minutes, allow to sit for 8 hours, add following ingredients and start cycle.

milk	3 tbs.	¼ cup	⅓ cup
vegetable oil	2 tsp.	1 tbs.	1½ tbs.
molasses	3 tbs.	¼ cup	⅓ cup
salt	½ tsp.	1 tsp.	1 tsp.
sugar	1½ tbs.	2 tbs.	2½ tbs.
cumin, ground	⅓ tsp.	½ tsp.	¾ tsp.
fennel, ground	⅓ tsp.	½ tsp.	¾ tsp.

raisins	⅓ cup	½ cup	⅔ cup
orange rind	½ orange	1 orange	1 orange
or dried peel	1½ tsp.	2 tsp.	1 tbs.
rye flour	¾ cup	1 cup	1½ cups
white bread flour	¾ cup	1 cup	1½ cups
vital gluten	2 tsp.	2 tsp.	1 tbs.
water as needed			

BAHRAIN ONION OLIVE BREAD

Since the Middle East is one of the great olive growing areas of the world, this recipe from Greece and Cyprus is typical of what one finds in Bahrain, and it's good. A 3.8 oz. can of sliced ripe olives equals 1 cup. Onions provide moisture to the dough. Scrape the sides of the pan with a rubber spatula if necessary to help mix the ingredients initially. If using a slower culture, add an hour delay.

	1 lb.	**1½ lb.**	**2 lb.**
sourdough culture	1 cup	1½ cups	2 cups
white bread flour	¾ cup	1 cup	1½ cups

Knead for 5 minutes, allow to sit for 8 hours, add following ingredients and start cycle.

	1 lb.	**1½ lb.**	**2 lb.**
water	2 tbs.	3 tbs.	¼ cup
salt	½ tsp.	½ tsp.	1 tsp.
olive oil	1½ tsp.	2 tsp.	1 tbs.
onion, chopped	½ cup	¾ cup	1 cup
ripe olives, sliced	½ cup	¾ cup	1 cup
white bread flour	¾ cup	1¼ cups	1½ cups
water as needed			

CARAWAY RYE BREAD

There is no better combination than rye, caraway and sourdough. This Austrian recipe uses the first sourdough culture that we discovered in Europe.This is a mildly heavy dough and will do better with the addition of vital gluten. A fast culture will leaven this nicely on a French, whole wheat or basic white cycle with no delay. A slower culture needs a 1-hour delay before the machine is started.

	1 lb.	1½ lb.	2 lb.
sourdough culture	1½ cups	2 cups	3 cups
white bread flour	¾ cup	1 cup	1½ cups

Knead for 5 minutes, allow to sit for 8 hours, add following ingredients and start cycle.

	1 lb.	1½ lb.	2 lb.
water	⅓ cup	½ cup.	⅔ cup
salt	½ tsp.	1 tsp.	1 tsp.
caraway seeds	2 tsp.	1 tbs.	1½ tbs.
vital gluten	1 tsp.	2 tsp.	1 tbs.
rye flour	¾ cup	1 cup	1½ cups
white bread flour	¾ cup	1 cup	1½ cups
water as needed			

EGYPTIAN WHOLE WHEAT KAMUT BREAD

Kamut with white flour rises very well. Kamut with whole wheat flour, on our test, rose even better! Use the French bread or whole wheat cycle.

	1 lb.	**1¼ lb.**	**1½ lb.**
sourdough culture	1 cup	1½ cups	2 cups
white bread flour	½ cup	¾ cup	1 cup

Knead for 5 minutes, allow to sit for 8 hours, add following ingredients and start cycle.

water	¼ cup	⅓ cup	½ cup
salt	½ tsp.	½ tsp.	1 tsp.
molasses	1½ tsp.	2 tsp.	1 tbs.
vegetable oil	1½ tsp.	2 tsp.	1 tbs.
brown sugar	1½ tsp.	2 tsp.	1 tbs.
vital gluten	1 tsp.	1 tsp.	2 tsp.
kamut	½ cup	¾ cup	1 cup
whole wheat flour	½ cup	¾ cup	1 cup
water as needed			

AUSTRIAN WHOLE SPELT BREAD

This recipe uses the whole grain spelt flour. (Purity Foods graciously supplied Ed with samples of Vita-Spelt white and whole grain flours.) Although the flour in this recipe is about one-third whole grain spelt, it rose well with a slow culture in programmable machines. If using a fast culture, use the French bread cycle.

	1 lb.	**1¼ lb.**	**1½ lb.**
sourdough culture	1 cup	1½ cups	2 cups
white bread flour	½ cup	½ cup	¾ cup

Knead for 5 minutes, allow to sit for 8 hours, add following ingredients and start cycle.

water	2 tbs.	3 tbs.	¼ cup
salt	½ tsp.	½ tsp.	1 tsp.
sugar	1½ tsp.	2 tsp.	1 tbs.
vegetable oil	1½ tsp.	2 tsp.	1 tbs.
anise seeds	½ tsp.	½ tsp.	1 tsp.
vital gluten	1 tsp.	2 tsp.	2 tsp.
whole spelt flour	¾ cup	1⅛ cups	1½ cups
white bread flour	¼ cup	¾ cup	¾ cup
water as needed			

CHEESE ONION BREAD

This is a simply delicious bread, but a real challenge to bake. Both the cheese and onions add an increment of water that is difficult to estimate. During the initial kneading, the dough appears far too stiff. Don't add water at this point unless the machine sounds like it is really struggling (in which case, as it may harm the motor, add water, but add flour during the second kneading). As kneading and resting occur, the cheese will begin to melt and the true consistency becomes more apparent. When the second knead is in progress, evaluate the paddle consistency and add water (or flour) as indicated, cautiously. It is also somewhat tricky to get a good initial mix of the cheese and onions. We found that it helped to turn off the machine and use a rubber spatula to break up the ingredients by hand. Then restart the machine mixing. Use a French bread cycle.

	1 lb.	1¼ lb.	1½ lb.
sourdough culture	¾ cup	1⅛ cups	1½ cups
white bread flour	½ cup	¾ cup	1 cup

Knead for 5 minutes, allow to sit for 8 hours, add following ingredients and start cycle.

onion, chopped	¼ cup	⅓ cup	½ cup
cheese, grated	¼ cup	⅓ cup	½ cup
vegetable oil	1½ tsp.	2 tsp.	1 tbs.
salt	½ tsp.	1 tsp.	1 tsp.
white bread flour	½ cup	¾ cup	1 cup
water as needed			

POTATO BREAD

Potato breads are popular everywhere. We sidestepped the boiling and mashing process by using potato flakes — instant mashed potatoes — and they worked very well. When we tested this in a Mr. Loaf (Seiko with slightly smaller baking pan than other 1½ lb. machines), it rose and rose, requiring multiple episodes of puncturing with a straightened paper clip to keep it in the pan. Maybe it was all that potato starch?

	1 lb.	**1¼ lb.**	**1½ lb.**
sourdough culture	¾ cup	1⅛ cups	1½ cups
white bread flour	½ cup	¾ cup	1 cup

Knead for 5 minutes, allow to sit for 8 hours, add following ingredients and start cycle.

vegetable oil	½ tbs.	2 tsp.	1 tbs.
milk, warm	2 tbs.	3 tbs.	¼ cup
salt	½ tsp.	½ tsp.	1 tsp.
potato flakes	½ cup	¾ cup	1 cup
white bread flour	½ cup	¾ cup	1 cup
water as needed			

FRENCH ONION BREAD

This combination of rye, sourdough and sautéed onions produces a blend of flavors found in few breads. The onion brings an increment of moisture to the recipe that suggests caution in adding additional water, so watch the paddle action carefully. If you use a slow culture, add all ingredients as normally, start the machine and allow to mix for 5 to 10 minutes. Then stop the machine and set it on the timer to start in 1 hour (1 hour added to the process). Sauté the onions in the olive oil prior to adding to the machine. Use a French bread cycle.

	1 lb.	1¼ lb.	1½ lb.
sourdough culture	1 cup	1½ cups	2 cups
white bread flour	½ cup	¾ cup	¾ cup

Knead for 5 minutes, allow to sit for 8 hours, add following ingredients and start cycle.

	1 lb.	1¼ lb.	1½ lb.
oive oil	1½ tsp.	2 tsp.	1 tbs.
onion, chopped	½ cup	¾ cup	1 cup
salt	½ tsp.	½ tsp.	1 tsp.
vital gluten	1 tsp.	2 tsp.	2 tsp.
rye flour	¾ cup	1⅛ cups	1½ cups
white bread flour	½ cup	½ cup	¾ cup
water as needed			

SWEDISH BREAD

This is another great bread that is an uncommon challenge to the bread machine baker, but worth it. The honey in this recipe produces a sticky texture that makes it difficult to evaluate the paddle consistency. In addition, it puts a sugar overload on the wild yeast and slows leavening. We suggest trying it in a programmable machine with a long last rise. If you don't have the machine, use the dough cycle and make pan loaves that can rise until you're ready to bake them. In our test, the honey produced an extremely dark crust, so set your oven for 350°. Very sticky doughs, as this one, sometimes cause the dough paddle to dislodge in the machine. You can spot this in an instant, since the dough just sits in the pan and quivers. If this happens you can reset the blade, but it's messy. Scrape the sides of the pan with a rubber spatula if necessary to help get the dough going. Measure the vegetable oil and then rub it into the cup in which you measure the honey — that way the honey slides out of the cup easily. We recommend using the vital gluten for best texture. Use the French bread cycle.

	1 lb.	**1½ lb.**	**2 lb.**
sourdough culture	1 cup	1½ cups	2 cups
white bread flour	½ cup	¾ cup	1 cup

Knead for 5 minutes, allow to sit for 8 hours, add following ingredients and start cycle.

	1 lb.	**1½ lb.**	**2 lb.**
vegetable oil	1½ tsp.	2 tsp.	1 tbs.
salt	½ tsp.	½ tsp.	1 tsp.
honey	¼ cup	⅓ cup	½ cup
fennel seeds	1½ tsp.	2 tsp.	1 tbs.
vital gluten	1½ tsp.	1 tbs.	1 tbs.
rye flour	1 cup	1½ cups	2 cups
water as needed			

ONION RYE BREAD

The Austrians are famous for their delicious rye breads. The recipe produces a moderately heavy dough requiring an aggressive fast culture. If you use the Austrian or a slow sourdough, the last rise should be at least 2 hours, or use the dough cycle and let it rise as long as necessary. Use the French bread cycle.

	1 lb.	**1½ lb.**	**2 lb.**
sourdough culture	1½ cups	2 cups	3 cups
white bread flour	⅔ cup	¾ cup	1 cup

Knead for 5 minutes, allow to sit for 8 hours, add following ingredients and start cycle.

	1 lb.	**1½ lb.**	**2 lb.**
milk	3 tbs.	¼ cup	⅓ cup
salt	½ tsp.	1 tsp.	1 tsp.
sugar	1½ tbs.	2 tbs.	2½ tbs.
butter	½ tbs.	1 tbs.	1½ tbs.
onion, raw, chopped	⅓ cup	½ cup	⅔ cup
caraway seeds	2 tsp.	1 tbs.	1⅓ tbs.
vital gluten	1 tbs.	1 tbs.	1½ tbs.
rye flour	1⅛ cups	1½ cups	2¼ cups
white bread flour	½ cup	¾ cup	1¼ cups
water as needed			

PUMPERNICKEL RYE BREAD

Strictly speaking, pumpernickel is rye meal, but it is often unavailable even in natural food stores. Rye comes in grades including white, medium, dark and rye meal. We used dark rye for pumpernickel. Since it is poor in gluten, it produces a heavy, sticky dough, so add vital gluten. It is a little difficult to judge consistency so add water with caution. Use the French bread cycle with a fast culture.

	1 lb.	**1½ lb.**	**2 lb.**
sourdough culture	1½ cups	2 cups	3 cups
white bread flour	¾ cup	1 cup	1¼ cups

Knead for 5 minutes, allow to sit for 8 hours, add following ingredients and start cycle.

milk	⅓ cup	½ cup	⅔ cup
salt	¾ tsp.	1 tsp.	1½ tsp.
sugar	2 tsp.	1 tbs.	1⅓ tbs.
butter	½ tbs.	1 tbs.	1½ tbs.
vital gluten	1½ tsp.	2 tsp.	1 tbs.
dark rye flour	1⅛ cups	1½ cups	2¼ cups
white bread flour	½ cup	⅔ cup	1¼ cups
water as needed			

DARK PUMPERNICKEL BREAD

*We used the same dark rye in this recipe as in the **Pumpernickel Rye**. The "dark" is supplied by the whole wheat flour and this dough is significantly heavier. When we tested it in the Zojirushi S-15 we used vital gluten and planned for a long rise. At the end of 2 hours the dough was within ½ inch of the pan top and we couldn't resist giving it more time. An hour later it was still within a half inch of the top and when the bake was started, it even retreated slightly. We concluded it is better to bake it after a 2-hour rise or on the normal French bread or whole wheat cycle. We recommend using the vital gluten. Use pumpernickel flour in place of the rye — if you can find it. Use a French bread cycle.*

	1 lb.	1½ lb.	2 lb.
sourdough culture	1½ cups	2 cups	3 cups
white bread flour	½ cup	⅔ cup	1 cup

Knead for 5 minutes, allow to sit for 8 hours, add following ingredients and start cycle.

salt	½ tsp.	½ tsp.	1 tsp.
sugar	1½ tbs.	2 tbs.	3 tbs.
milk	⅓ cup	½ cup	⅔ cup
vegetable oil	2 tsp.	1 tbs.	1⅓ tbs.
caraway seed	2 tsp.	1 tbs.	1⅓ tbs.
vital gluten	1 tbs.	1 tbs.	1½ tbs.
whole wheat flour	¾ cup	1 cup	1½ cups
dark rye flour	1⅛ cups	1½ cups	2¼ cups
water as needed			

HAM RYE BREAD

This isn't quite the same as having a slice of ham between two slices of rye, but it is an excellent combination that is awfully hard to beat. When we tested this one in Mr. Loaf we had to control the dough, as it came over the top repeatedly. Note that the recipe has the equivalent of 4 cups of flour for the large size, and even though one was rye, it would have been better mannered in a bigger pan. If you experience this problem, try a smaller recipe size. Use the French bread cycle.

	1 lb.	**1¼ lb.**	**1½ lb.**
sourdough culture	1 cup	1½ cups	2 cups
white bread flour	½ cup	¾ cup	1 cup

Knead for 5 minutes, allow to sit for 8 hours, add following ingredients and start cycle.

milk	2 tbs.	3 tbs.	¼ cup
sugar	1½ tsp.	2 tsp.	1 tbs.
vegetable oil	1½ tsp.	2 tsp.	1 tbs.
ham, chopped	¼ cup	⅓ cup	½ cup
caraway seeds	1½ tsp.	2 tsp.	1 tbs.
vital gluten	1 tsp.	2 tsp.	2 tsp.
rye flour	½ cup	¾ cup	1 cup
white bread flour	⅓ cup	½ cup	⅔ cup
water as needed			

AUSTRIAN WHEAT BREAD

This Austrian whole wheat recipe adds a touch of anise for a delightful and different rye bread. Use the French bread cycle.

	1 lb.	1½ lb.	2 lb.
sourdough culture	1½ cups	2 cups	2½ cups
white bread flour	¾ cup	1 cup	1⅛ cups

Knead for 5 minutes, allow to sit for 8 hours, add following ingredients and start cycle.

	1 lb.	1½ lb.	2 lb.
water	2 tbs.	3 tbs.	¼ cup
salt	½ tsp.	1 tsp.	1 tsp.
sugar	2 tsp.	1 tbs.	1⅓ tsp.
anise, ground	½ tsp.	½ tsp.	1 tsp.
vegetable oil	1½ tbs.	2 tbs.	2½ tbs.
vital gluten	1 tsp.	2 tsp.	2 tsp.
whole wheat flour	1⅛ cups	1½ cups	2 cups
white bread flour	½ cup	⅔ cup	1 cup
water as needed			

DILL RYE BREAD

This is another Austrian rye, but the dill offers an interesting twist — in the right direction — especially with sourdough. This rises beautifully on any basic white cycle, but use the French bread cycle if you have it.

	1 lb.	1¼ lb.	1½ lb.
sourdough culture	1 cup	1½ cups	2 cups
white bread flour	½ cup	¾ cup	1 cup

Knead for 5 minutes, allow to sit for 8 hours, add following ingredients and start cycle.

salt	½ tsp.	½ tsp.	1 tsp.
water	2 tbs.	3 tbs.	¼ cup
vegetable oil	1½ tsp.	2 tsp.	1 tbs.
caraway seeds	1½ tsp.	2 tsp.	1 tbs.
dill seeds	½ tsp.	½ tsp.	1 tsp.
vital gluten	1 tsp.	2 tsp.	2 tsp.
rye flour	½ cup	¾ cup	1 cup
white bread flour	½ cup	¾ cup	1 cup
water as needed			

RAISIN RYE BREAD

This Austrian blend of rye, raisins, and sourdough is a tasty treat, especially good for morning toast. This rises moderately well (just below or equal to the lip of the pan) on a basic white or French bread cycle. You should consider the dough cycle with the option for a longer rise if using a slow culture.

	1 lb.	**1¼ lb.**	**1½ lb.**
sourdough culture	1 cup	1½ cups	2 cups
white bread flour	½ cup	¾ cup	1 cup

Knead for 5 minutes, allow to sit for 8 hours, add following ingredients and start cycle.

water	2 tbs.	3 tbs.	¼ cup
salt	½ tsp.	½ tsp.	1 tsp.
sugar	1½ tsp.	2 tsp.	1 tbs.
vegetable oil	1½ tsp.	2 tsp.	1 tbs.
raisins	½ cup	¾ cup	1 cup
vital gluten	1 tsp.	2 tsp.	2 tsp.
rye flour	½ cup	¾ cup	1 cup
white bread flour	⅓ cup	½ cup	⅔ cup
water as needed			

COCOA RYE BREAD

Cocoa rye is out of Germany. The cocoa addition offers a unique flavor and produces a super dark bread. Use a French or basic white cycle.

	1 lb.	**1½ lb.**	**2 lb.**
sourdough culture	1½ cups	2 cups	2½ cups
white bread flour	¾ cup	1 cup	1⅓ cups

Knead for 5 minutes, allow to sit for 8 hours, add following ingredients and start cycle.

	1 lb.	**1½ lb.**	**2 lb.**
water	3 tbs.	¼ cup	⅓ cup
salt	½ tsp.	1 tsp.	1 tsp.
sugar	2 tsp.	1 tbs.	1⅓ tbs.
vegetable oil	2 tsp.	1 tbs.	1⅓ tbs.
cocoa	3 tbs.	¼ cup	⅓ cup
caraway seeds	2 tsp.	1 tbs.	1⅓ tbs.
vital gluten	2 tsp.	2 tsp.	1 tbs.
rye flour	1⅛ cups	1½ cups	1¾ cups
white bread flour	½ cup	⅔ cup	¾ cup
water as needed			

EGYPTIAN RYE KAMUT BREAD

We used the Red Sea culture at its leavening peak with this moderately heavy dough. Kamut is a whole grain flour and combined with rye needs an aggressive (fast) wild yeast to lift it. It did an excellent job and we gave it a high rating.

	1 lb.	**1¼ lb.**	**1½ lb.**
sourdough culture	¾ cup	1⅛ cups	1½ cups
white bread flour	½ cup	¾ cup	1 cup

Knead for 5 minutes, allow to sit for 8 hours, add following ingredients and start cycle.

water	2 tbs.	3 tbs.	¼ cup
salt	½ tsp.	½ tsp.	1 tsp.
vegetable oil	1½ tsp.	2 tsp.	1 tbs.
sugar	1 tbs.	1½ tbs.	2 tbs.
fennel seeds	1½ tsp.	2 tsp.	1 tbs.
caraway seeds	1½ tsp.	2 tsp.	1 tbs.
vital gluten	2 tsp.	1 tbs.	1⅓ tbs.
rye flour	½ cup	¾ cup	1 cup
kamut	½ cup	¾ cup	1 cup
water as needed			

AUSTRIAN RYE SPELT BREAD

This European recipe using spelt combines it with rye with excellent results. This rather heavy dough needs a long last rise time (90 minutes). This recipe uses the white spelt flour as opposed to the whole grain version.

	1 lb.	1¼ lb.	2 lb.
sourdough culture	1 cup	1½ cups	2 cups
white bread flour	½ cup	¾ cup	1 cup

Knead for 5 minutes, allow to sit for 8 hours, add following ingredients and start cycle.

	1 lb.	1¼ lb.	2 lb.
water	2 tbs.	3 tbs.	¼ cup
salt	½ tsp.	½ tsp.	1 tsp.
vegetable oil	1½ tsp.	2 tsp.	1 tbs.
sugar	1 tbs.	1½ tbs.	2 tbs.
fennel seeds	1½ tsp.	2 tsp.	1 tbs.
caraway seeds	1½ tsp.	2 tsp.	1 tbs.
vital gluten	2 tsp.	1 tbs.	1⅓ tbs.
rye flour	½ cup	¾ cup	1 cup
spelt flour	½ cup	¾ cup	1 cup
water as needed			

SOUR CREAM RYE BREAD

Rye, sour cream and sourdough. What a combination! This Austrian recipe is easy to make in any machine on the French or basic white cycle. The flavor is almost addictive.

	1 lb.	**1½ lb.**	**2 lb.**
sourdough culture	1⅛ cups	1½ cups	2 cups
white bread flour	⅔ cup	¾ cup	1⅛ cups

Knead for 5 minutes, allow to sit for 8 hours, add following ingredients and start cycle.

	1 lb.	**1½ lb.**	**2 lb.**
salt	½ tsp.	1 tsp.	1 tsp.
sugar	1½ tbs.	2 tbs.	3 tbs.
vegetable oil	½ tbs.	1 tbs.	1 tbs.
sour cream	⅓ cup	½ cup	⅔ cup
caraway seeds	2 tsp.	1 tbs.	1⅓ tbs.
vital gluten	2 tsp.	1 tbs.	1⅓ tbs.
rye flour	1½ cups	2 cups	2⅔ cups
white bread flour	½ cup	¾ cup	1 cup
water as needed			

OATMEAL BREAD

You may think of oatmeal as the modern health food, but this is a recipe right out of the "forty-niner" gold rush in California. The rolled oats produce a rough texture and increase the fiber content of this white bread much as do the whole wheat flours. It's an interesting bread and rates in our best twelve. Try it. A fast culture works best. If you use a slow culture, schedule a 1-hour delay before starting the French bread cycle. You may also use instant oats in this recipe.

	1 lb.	**1½ lb.**	**2 lb.**
sourdough culture	1½ cups	2 cups	2½ cups
white bread flour	1⅛ cups	1¼ cups	1¾ cups

Knead for 5 minutes, allow to sit for 8 hours, add following ingredients and start cycle.

	1 lb.	**1½ lb.**	**2 lb.**
salt	½ tsp.	1 tsp.	1 tsp.
brown sugar	2 tsp.	1 tbs.	1½ tbs.
rolled oats	¾ cup	1 cup	1⅓ cups
white bread flour	¾ cup	1¼ cups	1½ cups
water as needed			

LIGHT AUSTRIAN RYE BREAD

This Austrian recipe rises very well and the blend of rye and caraway seeds with the sourdough flavor produces a delicious combination which is lighter than most rye breads. The recipe suggests the French bread cycle as it provides longer leavening before baking. Try using a fast culture and a delay of 1 hour before starting the cycle. We successfully baked this bread in the regular cycle of some machines with as little as a 55-minute rise time before baking. With a slow culture you should consider using the dough cycle with as much time for leavening as required.

	1 lb.	**1½ lb.**	**2 lb.**
sourdough culture	1½ cups	2 cups	2½ cups
white bread flour	¾ cup	1 cup	1¼ cups

Knead for 5 minutes, allow to sit for 8 hours, add following ingredients and start cycle.

caraway seeds	2 tsp.	1 tbs.	1½ tbs.
salt	½ tsp.	1 tsp.	1 tsp.
vegetable oil	2 tsp.	1 tbs.	1⅓ tbs.
white bread flour	¾ cup	1 cup	1¼ cups
medium rye flour	¾ cup	1 cup	1¼ cups
water as needed			

FINNISH RYE BREAD

This rich heavy rye dough rises slowly and needs a relatively long leavening such as a last rise of 2 hours or longer. This means it does best in a programmable machine; otherwise, try using the dough cycle and allowing it to leaven as long as needed. If using a French, whole wheat or basic cycle, be sure to use the vital gluten.

	1 lb.	**1½ lb.**	**2 lb.**
sourdough culture	1½ cups	2 cups	2½ cups
white bread flour	¾ cup	1 cup	1¼ cups

Knead for 5 minutes, allow to sit for 8 hours, add following ingredients and start cycle.

milk	⅓ cup	½ cup	⅔ cup
salt	½ tsp.	1 tsp.	1-2 tsp.
caraway seeds	2 tsp.	1 tbs.	1⅓ tbs.
brown sugar	2 tbs.	3 tbs.	¼ cup
butter	½ tbs.	1 tbs.	1½ tbs.
vital gluten	2 tsp.	1 tbs.	1⅓ tbs.
rye flour	1½ cups	2 cups	2½ cups
water as needed			

JALAPEÑO RYE CHEESE BREAD

The cheese and jalapeños in a sourdough-rye matrix produce a flavor combination that is hard to beat. The cheese should be grated and lightly packed into the measuring cup. Scrape the sides of the pan if necessary to help get the dough going. Adjust the diced jalapeños to taste. Use the French bread cycle.

	1 lb.	**1½ lb.**	**2 lb.**
sourdough culture	1⅛ cups	1½ cups	2¼ cups
white bread flour	¾ cup	1 cup	1½ cups

Knead for 5 minutes, allow to sit for 8 hours, add following ingredients and start cycle.

butter	2 tsp.	1 tbs.	1½ tbs.
jalapeño cheese, grated	¾ cup	1 cup	1½ cups
jalapeños, diced	2	2	3
salt	½ tsp.	1 tsp.	1½ tsp.
sugar	2 tsp.	1 tbs.	1½ tbs.
vital gluten	2 tsp.	2 tsp.	1 tbs.
rye flour	¾ cup	1 cup	1½ cups
water as needed			

SLAVIC BLACK BREAD

This is a heavy, moist dark bread rich with molasses and sugar. It needs an aggressive fast culture and a long last rise (2 hours if you can) before baking. Be sure to use the vital gluten. Use dark rye flour if you can't find pumpernickel.

	1 lb.	1½ lb.	2 lb.
sourdough culture	1½ cups	2 cups	2½ cups
white bread flour	¾ cup	1 cup	1¼ cups

Knead for 5 minutes, allow to sit for 8 hours, add following ingredients and start cycle.

	1 lb.	1½ lb.	2 lb.
water	3 tbs.	¼ cup	⅓ cup
salt	½ tsp.	1 tsp.	1 tsp.
sugar	2 tsp.	1 tbs.	1 tbs.
molasses	1½ tbs.	2 tbs.	3 tbs.
vegetable oil	2 tsp.	1 tbs.	1½ tbs.
fennel, ground	½ tsp.	1 tsp.	1 tsp.
caraway seeds	1½ tsp.	2 tsp.	1 tbs.
vital gluten	1 tbs.	1½ tbs.	2 tbs.
whole wheat flour	¾ cup	1 cup	1¼ cups
pumpernickel flour	¾ cup	1 cup	1¼ cups
water as needed			

SUNFLOWER BREAD

This San Francisco recipe produces a light-textured, dark, nutty bread. Use raw sunflower seeds (kernels), not roasted, for best results. We had much success on all machines with last rises of between 75 and 90 minutes, (French, whole wheat or basic white).

	1 lb.	**1½ lb.**	**2 lb.**
sourdough culture	1½ cups	2 cups	2½ cups
white bread flour	½ cup	¾ cup	1 cup

Knead for 5 minutes, allow to sit for 8 hours, add following ingredients and start cycle.

salt	½ tsp.	1 tsp.	1 tsp.
sugar	2 tsp.	1 tbs.	1½ tbs.
butter	½ tbs.	1 tbs.	1½ tbs.
sunflower kernels	½ cup	¾ cup	scant 1 cup
vital gluten	½ tbs.	1 tbs.	1 tbs.
whole wheat flour	1⅛ cups	1½ cups	1¾ cups
white bread flour	⅔ cup	¾ cup	1 cup
water as needed			

AUTHENTIC SOURDOUGHS
DOUGH CYCLE

Any bread machine, programmable or not, will turn out perfect, authentic sourdough using the dough cycle. The real advantage to the dough cycle is that the machine does the initial, difficult kneading but you can then let the dough rise as long as necessary the second time (without machine-induced stir-downs) and pop it in the oven when it's ready. This is not only nice, but essential with the slow sourdough cultures, which may take a lot longer to leaven and develop that exquisite flavor than a machine will permit. You can use any culture, fast or slow, and time the entire process to fit the culture. The dough cycle also allows you to shape bread into traditional forms and shapes which have been enjoyed throughout history. There is something special and magical about the pockets of a pita bread or the braid of a challah. In this case, you are using the machine to do all the hard work of kneading and you simply derive the pleasure of shaping the bread.

HOW TO MAKE AUTHENTIC SOURDOUGH USING A DOUGH CYCLE

1. Remove the culture from the refrigerator.
2. Measure and then mix the culture and flour (listed first) in the machine for 5 to 10 minutes.
3. Feed remaining culture with equal parts of bread flour and water, proof at 85° for 45 to 60 minutes and then return to refrigerator.
4. Turn off the machine for 8 hours, and then:
5. Add the remaining ingredients and start the dough cycle.
6. Adjust the consistency with additional flour or water 1 tablespoon at a time. The consistency should be one smooth, round ball, not sticky or too moist. Add

flour, if necessary, during the first kneading (like Donna) in the machine, or you can add flour during the second kneading by hand (Ed's preference).

If your dough cycle is shorter than 1½ hours, allow the dough to sit in the warm machine for a full 1½ hours. On DAK or Welbilt ABM 100 machines with a full kneading, full hour rising and then another full kneading, turn the machine off after the first rise and do not allow the machine to knead a second time. You can turn the machine off after the initial kneading, set your oven timer for a 1-hour rise and then shape the dough. Other machines, such as the small Welbilt machines, have 2 kneadings on the dough cycle but they are only a few minutes apart. In this case, run the dough cycle as given but let the dough sit in the machine for a full 1½ hours (50-minute dough cycle plus 40 minutes extra).

After the completion of the dough cycle (1 kneading and 1 rising or about 1½ hours), knead in enough additional flour so the dough is not sticky and forms a satiny ball. If the dough is particularly moist (rye breads are notorious for this), it may require ½ cup to 1 cup of flour. Keep your bread board or counter and hands well floured.

You know the dough is ready to bake when you gently push on it with the tip of your finger and the indentation stays there. This is an indication that the bread is fully leavened. For fast cultures, the second rising may be as little as 30 or 45 minutes. For slow cultures, the second rising may take as long as 2 or 3 hours.

HINTS FOR BEST DOUGH MAKING TECHNIQUES

If you have a 1-lb. machine and a very active culture, you may want to do the initial step in a large plastic bowl. After the 8 hours, add all ingredients to the machine and run on the dough cycle as usual. This will prevent the potential of an overflow in the machine during the initial 8-hour proof. One-pound machines can handle this amount of dough on the dough cycle because it is not going through the second rise or baking. If you were to bake this large recipe in a 1-lb. machine, you would have serious overflow problems!

If you use a slow culture, let the dough rest for 1 hour in the machine after the dough cycle is complete. With a fast culture the dough may be shaped as soon as the cycle is finished.

If, during the first kneading, you adjusted the consistency to a fairly firm dough ball, you will add less flour during the second, manual kneading. In that case, just the floured counter will provide enough. If the dough is moist and sticky and is unable to hold any shape when removed from the pan, add enough flour during the second manual kneading until the dough is no longer sticky and forms a smooth satin ball. Usually from ½ to 1 cup of flour will be plenty. With both hands the dough is worked back and forth over the floured surface where it picks up a little additional flour with every motion. Form a rounded mass and push it in on the side away from you with the palm of your hand. Fold the edge back over the depression you have created, rotate the dough a quarter turn and repeat the process. Each time the dough picks up more flour and gradually loses its sticky surface to develop a satiny smooth sheen. Only the experience of trial and error will tell you when to quit.

Some machine bakers are intimidated by the very term "knead." But there really isn't much to it and most people enjoy it. It's hard to do it wrong; it's hard to do too much and a little experience will tell you when to quit. For some people, it's one of those mind-releasing exercises that is part of the innate satisfaction of making bread.

Keep in mind that sourdough does behave differently than other doughs. It relaxes more as it rises. If you obtained a dough that seemed just right during the dough cycle, don't be surprised to open the machine 1½ hours later and find a soft, sticky dough. Just add more flour during the second (manual) kneading as needed. If the dough isn't stiff enough, pan loaves will droop as they rise above the pan edge and French loaves will spread sideways instead of upward to form the plump loaf you'd like.

Most recipes specify letting the dough rise in a warm, draft-free location. If you have a proofing box (see page 11), this is the best place to let bread rise. Other locations may include an oven with a light on or a pan of hot water on the bottom shelf. Some people even put rising bread on top of a water heater.

CRUSTS

- Brushing with cold water just before baking produces a harder crust.

- French breads have a more chewy crust produced by placing a shallow pan of boiling water in the oven for the first 10 minutes of baking to simulate a steam oven.

- Brushing with melted butter or oil just before baking produces a softer crust.

- For a glossy hard crust, heat 1/2 cup water with 1 tsp. cornstarch to a boil while stirring. When cool, brush on the crust just before baking.

- Use a well beaten egg to form a golden crust or brush with milk for a deep brown crust.

- Heavy rounds of whole wheat and rye breads are sometimes brushed with flour just before cross-slashing to produce an attractive pattern.

PANS

You can save yourself many problems by using nonstick coated baking pans and baking sheets. If your pans are not nonstick, be sure to use a light coating of oil or margarine before baking. When the recipes do not specify pans, use the medium size —8 x 4 x 2 1/2 inches.

SOURDOUGH FRENCH BREAD

Because there is nothing in this bread to distract from the sourdough and because it is leavened only by wild sourdough and not commercial yeast, this is one of the most flavorful sourdough breads you will ever make. Any culture will successfully leaven this bread — the question is how long it will take.

2 cups sourdough culture
1½ cups white bread flour

Knead for 5 minutes, allow to sit for 8 hours, and then add:

1 tsp. salt
1½-2 cups white bread flour

Run the dough cycle. Then remove dough and shape to a long tubular shape only slightly smaller at the ends than in the middle. Place loaf on a baking sheet, seam down. Sprinkle surface with poppy or sesame seeds before making 3 or 4 slashes ¼-inch deep through crust with a razor blade or sharp knife. Let the loaf rise in a warm spot until it is at least double in volume, which will take from 1 to 3 hours depending on the speed of your culture. Bake at 350° for 35 to 45 minutes and cool on a wire rack.

BASIC SOURDOUGH

Using this recipe and making the bread on the dough cycle as described enables you to use any sourdough starter for an authentic sourdough without worrying about the timing of your machine. Start your sponge (the culture and 1½ cups white bread flour) before you go to bed and add remaining ingredients in the morning or start it before you go to work, add remaining ingredients before dinner and bake before you go to bed! Shape into a rectangular loaf or a round. The baking soda helps to leaven the sourdough but it also detracts slightly from the sourdough flavoring.

2 cups sourdough culture
1½ cups white bread flour

Knead for 5 minutes, allow to sit for 8 hours, and then add:

½ tsp. salt
1 tsp. sugar
1 tsp. baking soda
1½-2 cups white bread flour

Run the dough cycle. Then remove dough and knead into an oval or round ball of dough. Shape ball into an oblong somewhat shorter in length than the loaf pan and flatten it into an oval about ½-inch thick. Fold that oval in half lengthwise and pinch sides firmly together, forming a seam. Flour your hands as you pick up the loaf and smooth and shape surface until it looks like a small football. When you finish this process of flattening and shaping, the loaf should be slightly longer than the pan. Insert it in the pan with the seam down by arching the middle a bit and wedging it in place. Loaves tend to rise with more symmetry if the ends of the loaf butt up firmly against the ends of the pan.

Place loaf in a warm, draft-free location or proofing box at 85°. Allow to rise for 1 to 3 hours depending on the speed of your culture. The dough should be 1 inch above the lip of the pan. Bake at 350° for 50 to 55 minutes and cool on a wire rack.

HEARTY ROUND RYE

Because rye is low in gluten, this tends to be a dense loaf of bread and requires a longer rising time than breads with only white bread flour. A pan of water may be placed on the bottom rack of the oven during baking or the bread may be baked directly on a baking stone for a crispy crust.

2 cups sourdough culture   1½ cups white bread flour

Knead for 5 minutes, allow to sit for 8 hours, and then add:

½ tsp. salt   1 tbs. caraway (or anise or fennel) seed
1 tbs. vegetable oil   1 tbs. vital wheat gluten, optional
1 tbs. honey or molasses   1½ cups rye flour
1 tsp. dried orange peel, optional   0-½ cup white bread flour for texture

Run the dough cycle. Then remove dough and form into a round, slightly flat ball. Place seam side down on a well greased baking sheet. The round shape is maintained as it rises. Place in a 85° proofing box or other draft-free warm location to rise for 2 to 3½ hours, depending on the speed of your culture. Brush with water or an egg glaze and sprinkle with caraway seeds if desired. Bake at 350° for 35 to 45 minutes and cool on a wire rack.

KHOUBZ

This traditional pita bread recipe (see page 100) also makes a wonderful flatbread.

2 cups sourdough culture

1⅓ cups white bread flour

Knead for 5 minutes, allow to sit for 8 hours, and then add:

1 tsp. salt
1 tbs. sugar
1 tbs. olive oil
1 tsp. cumin
1 tsp. thyme

1 tsp. chili pepper or cayenne
¼ cup finely chopped onion
1⅓-1¾ cups white bread flour
1 tbs. olive oil

Run the dough cycle. Then remove dough and shape into a circle by pressing it gently onto a greased pizza or baking sheet. Place in a warm proofing box or other draft-free location to rise for 30 to 40 minutes. Thin dough will result in a crispy flatbread; thicker dough will result in a softer, chewier flatbread.

Using your fingers, make indentations in dough. If desired, place slivers of garlic, diced onions and pine nuts, chopped almonds or walnuts in the indentations. Brush dough with enough olive oil to cover the top. Bake in a preheated 500° oven for 20 to 25 minutes.

KHUBZ ARABI PITA

Pitas are the most distinctive breads of the Arab world. They offer an exceptional opportunity to taste the delicious flavors of sourdoughs from the Middle East where the process of leavened bread started some 5,000 to 10,000 years ago. Ed tested this with his Saudi Arabian culture. Whatever culture you use, the flavor comes through quite well. Makes 6 or 7.

2 cups sourdough culture
1½ cups white bread flour

Knead for 5 minutes, allow to sit for 8 hours, and then add:

1 tsp. salt
1½ tbs. sugar
1½ tbs. vegetable oil
1½-2 cups white bread flour

Run the dough cycle. Then remove dough and form as many large egg-sized round balls as the dough will produce (6 or 7). On a well floured board, use a roller to make flat rounds slightly less than 1/4-inch thick and 5 to 6 inches in diameter. It takes a little practice to change a round ball to a flat round, but it comes quickly. As the rounds are produced, flour each side lightly to prevent sticking and form 2 stacks with the rounds separated by wax paper. Do not put more than 3 or 4 rounds in each stack to prevent squashing the bottom ones. Let the stacks rise from 30 minutes to 1 hour at 85°.

Put an ungreased nonstick baking sheet or a pizza stone in your oven and preheat oven to 500°.

Transfer the rounds to a well floured bread board or baking sheet, one or two at a time, and with a spatula or pizza peel, slide them onto the heated baking sheet. Use care not to damage the surface of the rounds or they will not form a pouch.

Within about 2 minutes the rounds will begin to swell, usually from several different spots which blend rapidly to form a large central pouch. Continue baking until the pitas have browned slightly, about 7 minutes. Remove them from the oven and cool on a wire rack.

Be sure oven and baking sheet or stone have regained the 500° temperature between batches. It is the high temperature which provides the magic "puffs."

MANNAEESH (THYME PITAS)

Pitas are found in virtually every Arabian country. They are often eaten plain, but the pouch may be filled with native foods or seasonings. The herbs (omit the extra oil and sesame seeds) may be added to the dough itself for a flavorful, herbed pita instead of just the topping. Either way, the pitas are delicious. Makes 6 or 7 pitas.

2 cups sourdough culture   1⅓ cups white bread flour

Knead for 5 minutes, allow to sit for 8 hours, and then add:

1 tsp. salt   1 tbs. olive oil
1 tbs. sugar   1⅓-1¾ cups white bread flour

Follow the directions in the previous recipe, *Khubz Arabi Pita*, page 100. Brush the topping on just before baking.

TOPPING

3 tbs. olive oil   1 tsp. marjoram, ground
1 tsp. thyme   2 tbs. sesame seeds

Mix ingredients together.

BAHRAIN CHEESE BREAD

This is a Middle Eastern recipe discovered in Bahrain. The cream cheese filling permeates the entire bread. The sourdough, cheese and sesame seeds are an excellent combination that is easy to make.

2 cups sourdough culture   1½ cups white bread flour

Knead for 5 minutes, allow to sit for 8 hours, and then add:

1 tsp. salt   8 oz. cream cheese, softened
2 tbs. sugar   ——
1 tbs. vegetable oil   glaze: 1 egg, beaten
1½-2 cups white bread flour   sesame seeds

Run the dough cycle. Then remove dough, and on a lightly floured counter, roll into a rectangle about ½-inch thick. Add only enough flour to prevent dough from sticking. Spread softened cream cheese over dough rectangle, leaving 1 inch of margin clear. Jelly-roll up from the long side and pinch the bottom seam and ends together. Place on a greased baking sheet with seam down. Brush with egg and sprinkle with sesame seeds. Let rise in a warm, draft-free location (85°) for 1 to 2 hours, depending on the speed of the culture, until double in size. Bake at 375° for 40 to 45 minutes and cool on a wire rack.

EGG BRAIDS

Any sourdough culture from the slowest to the fastest can be used for these attractive breads, since they can rise until the baker decides it's time to bake.

2 cups sourdough culture   1½ cups white bread flour

Knead for 5 minutes, allow to sit for 8 hours, and then add:

1 tbs. butter or margarine   1½-2 cups white bread flour
½ cup warm milk   —
1 tsp. salt   glaze: one egg, beaten
1 tbs. sugar   sesame seeds
2 eggs

Run the dough cycle. Then remove dough, divide it into 3 equal portions and form 3 balls. Add flour only if necessary to keep dough from sticking. Shape each ball into a rope about 18 to 24 inches long and ½ to 1 inch in diameter. Use ropes to make a braid. You can start at one end and braid to the opposite end or start in the middle and braid in both directions. Let braid rise on a greased baking sheet for 1 to 3 hours depending on the speed of your culture. Brush surface with beaten egg, sprinkle with sesame seeds and bake in a preheated oven at 375° for 35 to 45 minutes until golden brown.

EGYPTIAN SEMIT

This is a Middle Eastern recipe for delicate bread rings flavored by sourdough and sesame seeds. Not quite a pretzel, but similar. This recipe makes from 10 to 15 rings.

2 cups sourdough culture   1⅓ cups white bread flour

Knead for 5 minutes, allow to sit for 8 hours, and then add:

1 tsp. salt   1⅓-1¾ cups white bread flour
1 tbs. sugar   —
¼ cup water   glaze: 1 egg, beaten
1 tbs. olive oil   sesame seeds

Run the dough cycle. Then remove dough and form as many egg-sized pieces (10-15) as dough will supply. Roll pieces between your hands to form ropes about 8 inches long, twisting occasionally. Then form into rings, pinching ends together. Place on a greased baking sheet, glaze with beaten egg and sprinkle with sesame seeds. Cover with a dry cloth and allow to rise for ½ hour to 1 hour with a fast culture, or 1 to 2 hours with a slow culture. Preheat oven to 450° and just before baking, pour boiling water into a pan at the bottom of the oven to form steam. Bake for 15 to 20 minutes and cool on baking sheet.

SOURDOUGH PRETZELS

These are similar to pretzels you buy on the street, but fresher and better. Bet you can't eat just one! They are best eaten fresh from the oven. If storing for later consumption, make sure they are well cooled prior to wrapping.

1 cup sourdough culture
1½ cups white bread flour

Knead for 5 minutes, allow to sit for 8 hours, and then add:

2 tbs. butter or margarine
2 tbs. sugar
½ tsp. salt
1½-1¾ cups white bread flour

Run the dough cycle. Then remove dough and form into egg-sized pieces (12 to 15). Roll each piece into a long rope, about 12 to 14 inches long. Tie each rope into a pretzel shape and place on a greased baking sheet or perforated pizza pan. Cover and allow to rise in a warm, draft-free location for 30 to 40 minutes.

BOILING SOLUTION

4 cups water
2 tbs. baking soda

glaze: 1 egg, beaten with 2 tbs. milk
kosher or coarse salt

While pretzels are rising, bring water and baking soda to boil in a large, nonaluminum pan. Gently place (by hand or slotted spoon) 2 or 3 pretzels at a time into water and cook for approximately 1 minute — no more. Remove pretzels gently from water and place on a greased baking sheet. Repeat this process until all pretzels have been bathed in water. Brush with egg glaze and sprinkle coarse salt on top. Bake in a preheated 425° oven for 15 to 18 minutes or until pretzels are crusty and well browned. The longer they cook, the crispier they are, but you don't want to burn them.

SOURDOUGH CRACKERS

These are incredibly easy to make and are well worth it. If you forget to prick the crackers with a fork or knife you will have puffy crackers but every bit as tasty. Cookie cutters may be used for fancy shapes and fun with kids —or for festive gifts. While poppy and/or sesame seeds are traditionally used for crackers, try amaranth or quinoa grains or even anise, fennel or caraway seeds! As a variation to the water wash with seeds, brush the crackers with honey or with olive oil. The longer they are baked, the crispier they are. For a softer cracker, bake until just done.

1 cup sourdough culture
1½ cups white bread flour

Knead for 5 minutes, allow to sit for 8 hours, and then add:

¼ cup water
2 tbs. sugar
½ tsp. salt
1½-1¾ cups white bread flour
—
water wash
seeds of choice

Run the dough cycle. Then remove dough and roll into a thin rectangle. Using a pizza wheel or sharp knife, cut rectangle into 16 squares and place on a greased baking sheet or perforated pizza pan. Cover and allow to rise in a warm, draft-free location for 30 to 40 minutes. Pierce each cracker with a fork or sharp knife, brush with cold water and sprinkle with seeds of your choice just before baking. Bake in a preheated 425° oven for 15 to 18 minutes or until golden brown.

KHOBZ

This Arabian whole wheat flat bread is a combination of a bread and a pancake. One is tempted to wonder if perhaps khobz represents an intermediate step in the historic development of leavened breads as we know them today. Try this recipe with the Saudi Arabian or a slower culture.

2 cups sourdough culture
1 tsp. salt
2⅔ cups whole wheat flour
water or flour as needed

Remove culture from refrigerator. Add all of the ingredients to the measured culture and mix in the machine for 10 to 15 minutes. (Feed remaining culture with equal parts of bread flour and water, proof for 45 to 60 minutes and then return to refrigerator.) Adjust the paddle consistency by adding flour or water 1 tablespoon at a time.

Turn off the machine for 8 hours, and then:

Run the dough cycle. Then remove dough and knead in enough (approximately ½ cup) bread flour until dough is smooth and elastic. Form 8 to 10 balls about 1½ inches in diameter. Flatten balls with a roller to 4-inch rounds.

Cover rounds with a dry cloth on a board or counter (do not stack) and allow to rise. If using a fast culture, allow to rise for about 30 minutes. If using a slow culture. rounds should be allowed to rise for 1 hour. Cook rounds 1 to 2 minutes on each side over direct heat on a heavy greased pan or griddle heated just short of smoking hot. Serve warm with honey.

PSOMI

This is a crusty Greek sourdough which differs from French sourdough by the addition of sugar and olive oil. The crust is produced by steam from boiling water in the first minutes of baking. Makes 2 loaves.

2 cups sourdough culture

1⅓ cups white bread flour

Knead for 5 minutes, allow to sit for 8 hours, and then add:

2 tbs. sugar
1 tsp. salt
1 tbs. olive oil

1⅓ -1¾ cups white bread flour
white corn meal, optional

Run the dough cycle. Then remove dough and divide into 2 equal portions. Shape into 2 long, tubular shapes only slightly smaller at the ends than in the middle. Place seam side down on a greased baking sheet sprinkled with white corn meal. Allow to rise at 85° for 1½ hours if using a fast culture or 2½ to 3 hours if using slow culture. Preheat oven to 400°. Just before baking, make 3 or 4 diagonal slashes ¼-inch deep in the crust. Immediately before baking, pour boiling water into a flat baking pan on the lowest level to create steam. Remove water after 15 minutes. Bake 40 to 45 minutes and cool on a wire rack.

BAHRAIN BREAD RING

Bread rings and braided pastries are common throughout the Middle East. This one from Bahrain is almost generic for the entire area. It produces a fine, light, delicious loaf.

2 cups sourdough culture   1½ cups white bread flour

Knead for 5 minutes, allow to sit for 8 hours, and then add:

1 tsp. salt   1½-2 cups white bread flour
2 tbs. sugar   —
1 tbs. olive oil   water wash
¼ cup water   sesame or poppy seeds

Run the dough cycle. Then remove dough and flatten by hand or with a roller into a large oval less than ¼-inch thick. Next, starting at one edge, roll the flat into a tight rope. Continue rolling back and forth with gentle pressure until rope is at least 24 inches long. As the final step, twist rope with multiple twists and join the two ends to form a ring. Place on a greased baking sheet. Allow to rise for 1 to 3 hours depending on the speed of the culture being used. Brush top with water and sprinkle with sesame or poppy seeds. Bake at 375° for 35 to 40 minutes and cool on baking sheet.

BAGUETTES

The baguette is a long, long chewy French loaf with a hard crust. In France, baguettes are always made with sourdough, and are two feet long. In the U.S., authentic sourdough baguettes are a rarity. Now you can easily bake your own the way they should be made. To make them as long as possible with your equipment and oven, measure your oven, pans and proofing box, if you use one, before you start.

2 cups sourdough culture
1¼ cups white bread flour

Knead for 5 minutes, allow to sit for 8 hours, and then add:

½ cup milk
1 tbs. vegetable oil
1 tsp. salt
1 tbs. sugar
1¼-1¾ cups white bread flour
—
egg glaze: 1 egg, beaten

Run the dough cycle. Then remove dough and form 3 balls of roughly equal size. Form a long narrow rope from each ball. Ropes should be as long as your baking sheet and about 1½ inches in diameter. Allow to rise on a greased baking sheet for 1 to 2 hours. If you arrange the ropes within 1 inch of each other and then separate them with narrow strips of waxed paper, they will support each other as they rise and have less tendency to flatten. Just before baking, brush with egg glaze and then make short diagonal slashes along the entire length. Leave waxed paper strips in place and bake in a preheated oven at 375° for 35 minutes. Cool on a wire rack. The waxed strips will help to separate the baguettes and can be removed when cool.

CHALLAH

Challah (sometimes pronounced HALLAH or HAL-LA) is a giant Jewish braid. Its rich yellow dough can be covered with various seeds, glazes and candied fruits. The sourdough flavor goes well with almost anything. The saffron or turmeric give the bread the well-known yellow color. Some people have been known to cheat and use yellow food coloring — heresy!

2 cups sourdough culture
1½ cups white bread flour

Knead for 5 minutes, allow to sit for 8 hours, and then add:

2 tbs. butter
½ cup milk
1 tsp. salt
2 tbs. sugar
pinch saffron (or turmeric)
2 eggs
1½-2 cups white bread flour

glaze: 1 egg, beaten
sesame seeds

Run the dough cycle. Then remove dough and divide into 4 equal balls and roll each ball into a rope about 20 inches long and 1 inch in diameter. To braid, pinch the 4 ropes together at one end and arrange them side by side on a greased baking sheet. Complete the braid by bringing the rope on the right over the one next to it, under the third one and over the last one. Repeat the process, always starting with the rope on the right, until the braid is complete. Pinch the ends together. Allow to rise on the baking sheet 1 to 2 hours depending on the speed of your culture. Brush with egg glaze and sprinkle with sesame or poppy seeds. Bake in a preheated oven 375° for 35 to 40 minutes and cool on baking sheet.

SAMOULI (WHITE BREAD STICKS)

These bread sticks are traditionally prepared as snacks or appetizers before Arab meals. They can be any length from quite short to as long as your baking sheet will accommodate. The sourdough flavor guarantees a bread stick better than you've ever snacked on before.

2 cups sourdough culture   1⅓ cups white bread flour

    Knead for 5 minutes, allow to sit for 8 hours, and then add:

1 tbs. sugar	—
1 tbs. vegetable oil	glaze: 1 egg, beaten
1⅓ -1¾ cups white bread flour	sesame or poppy seeds

    Run the dough cycle. Then remove dough and form into 4 equal balls. Roll each into a flat round about 18 inches in diameter and ⅛-inch thick. Slice rounds into quarters and roll into sticks from the wide end to the point. As each stick is completed, first brush it with the egg glaze, and then roll it in a pan of sesame or poppy seeds. Twist it several times. Allow twisted sticks to rise on a greased baking sheet for ½ to 1 hour with a fast culture or twice that long with a slow one. Bake for 15 to 20 minutes at 450° and cool on baking sheet.

DINNER ROLLS

This is the only recipe in the book that recommends all-purpose flour. These softer flours produce a lighter roll than do bread flours. This recipe can produce many kinds of rolls with different names and shapes. This one is intended for Parker House rolls. Makes 12 to 15 rolls.

2 cups sourdough culture   1½ cups all purpose flour

Knead for 5 minutes, allow to sit for 8 hours, and then add:

2 tbs. butter   1 tsp. salt
1 egg   ¼ cup milk
1 tbs. sugar   1½-2 cups all purpose flour

Run the dough cycle. Then remove dough and form into a ball. With a roller, flatten it to about ½-inch thickness. Use a round cutter to make as many 3-inch rounds as the dough will produce. With a table knife, lightly crease each round across the middle and fold the two halves together, securing them with a light pinch. Allow to rise on a greased baking sheet for ½ to 1 hour. Bake at 400° for 20 to 25 minutes or until brown. Cool on wire racks.

CINNAMON ROLLS

This all-time breakfast favorite is not only easy to make but, with sourdough, better than ever. Makes 12.

2 cups sourdough culture
1½ cups white bread flour

Knead for 5 minutes, allow to sit for 8 hours, and then add:

¼ cup milk	1½-2 cups white bread flour
1 tsp. vanilla	—
1 tsp. salt	2 tbs. melted butter to brush on dough
2 tbs. sugar	

Run the dough cycle. Then remove dough and roll into a large rectangle about ½-inch thick. Brush with melted butter and sprinkle with sugar-cinnamon mixture and raisins. Roll up rectangle from long side and cut into 1-inch-thick rolls. Place rolls on a greased baking sheet close together and allow to rise at 85° for 1 to 2 hours. Bake at 400° for 25 to 30 minutes. While hot, drizzle with powdered sugar glaze.

FILLING

2 tbs. sugar
2 tsp. cinnamon

1 cup raisins

    Mix ingredients together.

GLAZE

1 cup powdered sugar
4 tsp. hot milk

$\frac{1}{2}$ tsp. vanilla

    Mix ingredients together.

CINNAMON RAISIN NUT BREAD

Made with sourdough, this popular recipe is different and delicious. Makes 2 loaves.

2 cups sourdough culture

1½ cups white bread flour

Knead for 5 minutes, allow to sit for 8 hours, and then add:

1 tbs. butter
½ cup warm milk
1 tsp. salt

1 tbs. sugar
1 tbs. cinnamon
2-2½ cups white bread flour

FILLING

2 tbs. cinnamon
½ cup sugar

½ cup chopped walnuts
½ cup raisins

Run the dough cycle. Then remove dough and divide in half. Grease 2 loaf pans. Roll dough into rectangles the width of pans and ½-inch thick. The bread board should be well floured to prevent sticking. Spread half of the filling on each rectangle. Roll up from the narrow side to form a tight loaf and pinch the seams and ends together. Place in pans and allow to rise 1 to 1½ hours with a fast culture or 2 to 3 hours with a slow one. When dough is 1 inch above the lip of the pan, bake in a preheated oven at 350° for 55 to 60 minutes. Cool on wire racks.

HAMBURGER BUNS

The all-American favorite tastes better in sourdough and you can make it with endless additions: chopped onions, sunflower seeds, poppy seeds, etc. Try these with different sourdough cultures for real flavor treats. Makes 12 to 15.

2 cups sourdough culture
1½ cups white bread flour

Knead for 5 minutes, allow to sit for 8 hours, and then add:

2 tbs. butter
¼ cup milk
1 egg
1 tsp. salt
2 tbs. sugar

1½-2 cups white bread flour
—
glaze: 1 egg, beaten
sesame or poppy seeds

Run the dough cycle. Then remove dough and form it into a ball. With a roller, flatten dough into a large oval about 1 inch thick. Use a sharp round cutter to form as many 4-inch rounds as the dough will produce. Place on a greased baking sheet and allow to rise for 1 to 1½ hours with a fast culture and 2 to 2½ hours with a slow one. Brush with beaten egg glaze and sprinkle with sesame seeds. Bake at 350° for 15 to 18 minutes or until brown. Cool on a wire rack.

POPPY SEED ROLLS

This light French roll that you will enjoy for any meal is a variation of the dinner roll recipe. Makes 12 to 15.

2 cups sourdough culture
1½ cups white bread flour

Knead for 5 minutes, allow to sit for 8 hours, and then add:

2 tbs. vegetable oil
1 tsp. salt
1 tbs. sugar
¼ cup milk
1 egg

1½-2 cups white bread flour
—
glaze: 1 egg, beaten with 2 tbs. milk
poppy seeds

Run the dough cycle. Then remove dough and divide into 10 equal balls. Flatten into oval rolls and place on a greased baking sheet. Brush with glaze and sprinkle with poppy seeds. Allow to rise for 1 to 2 hours. Bake at 425° for 20 to 25 minutes.

"PUSHBUTTON" SOURDOUGHS
ADDING COMMERCIAL YEAST TO SOURDOUGH RECIPES

Using commercial yeast in addition to wild sourdough yeast enables bread machine users to make sourdough bread with ease. There is no doubt that using yeast in combination with wild sourdough yeast diminishes the flavor of the sourdough. It is for this reason that Ed is vehemently opposed to using *any* commercial yeast in combination with sourdough. The recipes in this chapter were developed and tested by Donna for ease and greater reliability in the machine. These loaves do, nontheless, retain a sourdough flavor.

DIRECTIONS FOR SOURDOUGHS WITH THE ADDITION OF COMMERCIAL YEAST

1. Remove the entire culture from the refrigerator.
2. Discard (or give to a friend) 1 cup of the culture and replace it with 1 cup of bread flour and a scant cup of water. The consistency of the starter should be similar to a thick pancake batter.
3. Warm the starter in a proofing box or other warm, draft-free location at 85° for about 8 hours.
4. Measure the required starter for your recipe and add it and all other ingredients to the machine in the normal way. (DAK and Welbilt machine owners should read recipes in this book from the bottom up, beginning with yeast.)
5. Feed or replenish your sourdough starter with 1 to 2 cups of bread flour and an equal amount of water. Warm the culture for 45 minutes at 85° and then return to the refrigerator.

SOURDOUGH FRENCH BREAD

This basic sourdough recipe is made without fat.

	1 lb.	**1½ lb.**	**2 lb.**
water	⅓ cup	½ cup	⅔ cup
sourdough culture	⅔ cup	¾ cup	1 cup
sugar	1 tbs.	1½ tbs.	2 tbs.
salt	½ tsp.	¾ tsp.	1 tsp.
white bread flour	2 cups	3 cups	3½ cups
yeast	1 tsp.	1½ tsp.	2 tsp.
water or flour	1 tablespoon at a time if and as needed to obtain a smooth dough ball		

RECOMMENDED CYCLE   basic white, French

BASIC WHITE SOURDOUGH

*The addition of butter or margarine in this basic bread gives it a little softer crumb than **Sourdough French Bread**, page 128.*

	1 lb.	1½ lb.	2 lb.
water	¼ cup	⅓ cup	½ cup
sourdough culture	⅔ cup	¾ cup	1 cup
margarine or butter	1 tbs.	1½ tbs.	2 tbs.
sugar	1 tbs.	1½ tbs.	2 tbs.
salt	½ tsp.	¾ tsp.	1 tsp.
white bread flour	2 cups	3 cups	3½ cups
yeast	1 tsp.	1½ tsp.	2 tsp.
water or flour	1 tablespoon at a time if and as needed to obtain a smooth dough ball		

RECOMMENDED CYCLE   basic white, French

WHEAT SOURDOUGH

This bread, lightly flavored with whole wheat, accompanies anything and makes great sandwiches.

	1 lb.	1½ lb.	2 lb.
sourdough culture	1 cup	1½ cups	1¾ cups
water	¼ cup	⅓ cup	⅜ cup (3 oz.)
margarine or butter	1 tbs.	1½ tbs.	2 tbs.
sugar	1 tbs.	1½ tbs.	2 tbs.
salt	½ tsp.	¾ tsp.	1 tsp.
whole wheat flour	½ cup	¾ cup	1 cup
white bread flour	2 cups	3 cups	3½ cups
yeast	1 tsp.	1½ tsp.	2 tsp.
water or flour	1 tablespoon at a time if and as needed to obtain a smooth dough ball		

RECOMMENDED CYCLE   basic white, French

CORNMEAL SOURDOUGH

The cornmeal subtly flavors this bread. Use either white, yellow or blue cornmeal.
The gluten helps to give a lighter texture with a higher rise and is purely optional.

	1 lb.	**1½ lb.**	**2 lb.**
sourdough culture	1 cup	1½ cups	1¾ cups
water	2 tbs.	3 tbs.	¼ cup
margarine or butter	1 tbs.	1½ tbs.	2 tbs.
sugar	1 tbs.	1½ tbs.	2 tbs.
salt	½ tsp.	¾ tsp.	1 tsp.
cornmeal	¼ cup	⅓ cups	½ cup
white bread flour	2 cups	3 cups	3½ cups
vital gluten, optional	1 tbs.	1½ tbs.	2 tbs.
yeast	1 tsp.	1½ tsp.	2 tsp.
water or flour	1 tablespoon at a time if and as needed to obtain a smooth dough ball		

RECOMMENDED CYCLE   basic white, French

SPICY CORNMEAL SOURDOUGH

The onion adds moisture to this dough depending on how fresh it is. The vital gluten is optional for a lighter texture.

	1 lb.	**1½ lb.**	**2 lb.**
sourdough culture	1 cup	1½ cups	1¾ cups
diced onion	2 tbs.	3 tbs.	¼ cup
margarine or butter	1 tbs.	1½ tbs.	2 tbs.
cayenne	½ tsp.	¾ tsp.	1 tsp.
or crushed red pepper flakes	1 tsp.	1½ tsp.	2 tsp.
sugar	1 tbs.	1½ tbs.	2 tbs.
salt	½ tsp.	¾ tsp.	1 tsp.
cornmeal	¼ cup	⅓ cup	½ cup
white bread flour	2 cups	3 cups	3½ cups
vital gluten, optional	1 tbs.	1½ tbs.	2 tbs.
yeast	1 tsp.	1½ tsp.	2 tsp.
water or flour	1 tablespoon at a time if and as needed to obtain a smooth dough ball		

RECOMMENDED CYCLE basic white, French

HONEY NUT OATMEAL SOURDOUGH

This flavorful loaf makes great French toast with a little cinnamon. Walnut oil (found in large grocery stores) adds extra flavor, but vegetable oil may be substituted.

	1 lb.	1½ lb.	2 lb.
sourdough culture	⅔ cup	¾ cup	1 cup
water	⅓ cup	⅜ cup	½ cup
walnut oil	1 tbs.	1½ tbs.	2 tbs.
honey	2 tbs.	3 tbs.	¼ cup
salt	½ tsp.	¾ tsp.	1 tsp.
oats	½ cup	⅔ cup	¾ cup
white bread flour	2 cups	3 cups	3½ cups
yeast	1 tsp.	1½ tsp.	2 tsp.
water or flour	1 tablespoon at a time if and as needed to obtain a smooth dough ball		
*chopped walnuts	⅓ cup	½ cup	½ cup

RECOMMENDED CYCLE   raisin or basic white

*Add nuts at the beep or appropriate time for your machine.

MAPLE WALNUT SOURDOUGH

This is an outstanding loaf. If your machine is prone to "the doughy blues," cut the amount of nuts in half. Yes, the water amount for the medium and the large recipe are the same. As usual, however, watch the dough and adjust water or flour if necessary. Vegetable oil may be used in place of the walnut oil if desired.

	1 lb.	1½ lb.	2 lb.
water	½ cup	⅔ cup	⅔ cup
sourdough culture	⅔ cup	¾ cup	1 cup
walnut oil	1 tbs.	1½ tbs.	2 tbs.
maple syrup	1 tbs.	1½ tbs.	2 tbs.
salt	½ tsp.	¾ tsp.	1 tsp.
white bread flour	2 cups	3 cups	3½ cups
yeast	1 tsp.	1½ tsp.	2 tsp.
water or flour	1 tablespoon at a time if and as needed to obtain a smooth dough ball		
*chopped walnuts	⅓ cup	½ cup	⅔ cup

RECOMMENDED CYCLE   sweet, raisin or basic white
*Add nuts at the beep or appropriate time for your machine.

WHOLE GRAIN SOURDOUGH

Orange or apple juice concentrate (thawed) may be substituted for the vegetable oil if desired. Whole grains vary tremendously in the absorption of water so watch the dough and adjust as necessary. Use either freshly milled or commercially packaged whole wheat for this one. Gluten was used in all test loaves but, as usual, is an optional ingredient.

	1 lb.	**1½ lb.**	**2 lb.**
water	⅓ cup	½ cup	¾ cup
sourdough culture	¾ cup	1 cup	1¼ cups
vegetable oil	1 tbs.	1½ tbs.	2 tbs.
honey	2 tbs.	3 tbs.	4 tbs.
salt	½ tsp.	¾ tsp.	1 tsp.
whole wheat flour	2½ cups	3⅓ cups	4¼ cups
vital gluten	1½ tsp.	2 tsp.	1 tbs.
yeast	1½ tsp.	2 tsp.	2½ tsp.
water or flour	1 tablespoon at a time if and as needed to obtain a smooth dough ball		

RECOMMENDED CYCLE   whole wheat, sweet or basic white

SQUAW SOURDOUGH BREAD

Squaw bread was made by early New England colonists and was probably leavened with sourdoughs. Add the raisins (plumped in boiling water if you desire) at the beginning of the cycle with all other ingredients.

	1 lb.	1½ lb.	2 lb.
water	⅓ cup	½ cup	⅔ cup
sourdough culture	⅔ cup	¾ cup	1 cup
corn or vegetable oil	1 tbs.	1½ tbs.	2 tbs.
honey or molasses	1 tbs.	1½ tbs.	2 tbs.
raisins	¼ cup	⅓ cup	½ cup
salt	½ tsp.	¾ tsp.	1 tsp.
white bread flour	2 cups	3 cups	3½ cups
yeast	1 tsp.	1½ tsp.	2 tsp.
water or flour	1 tablespoon at a time if and as needed to obtain a smooth dough ball		
*sunflower kernels (or nuts)	¼ cup	⅓ cup	½ cup

RECOMMENDED CYCLE   raisin, sweet or basic white
*Add sunflower kernels at beep or appropriate time for your machine.

SOURDOUGH ONION RYE

The vital gluten is not necessary but it will give you a higher rising, lighter textured loaf. The combination of sourdough, onion and rye seems to blend in perfect harmony. Anise or fennel seeds may be used in place of the caraway for variation.

	1 lb.	**1½ lb.**	**2 lb.**
sourdough culture	1 cup	1½ cups	1¾ cups
vegetable oil	1 tbs.	1½ tbs.	2 tbs.
molasses	1 tbs.	1½ tbs.	2 tbs.
diced onion	2 tbs.	3 tbs.	¼ cup
caraway seeds	1½ tsp.	2 tsp.	1 tbs.
salt	½ tsp.	¾ tsp.	1 tsp.
rye flour	¾ cup	1 cup	1⅛ cups
white bread flour	1½ cups	2¼ cups	3 cups
vital gluten	1 tbs.	1½ tbs.	2 tbs.
yeast	1 tsp.	1½ tsp.	2 tsp.
water or flour	1 tablespoon at a time if and as needed to obtain a smooth dough ball		

RECOMMENDED CYCLE basic white, French

SCANDINAVIAN SOURDOUGH

Most of us think of rye flour in Scandinavian breads, but barley is another popular grain there. This recipe is adapted from one which is traced to the Middle Ages. This rises well — use the large recipe only in a full 2 lb. machine.

	1 lb.	1½ lb.	2 lb.
water	⅓ cup	½ cup	⅔ cup
sourdough culture	¾ cup	1 cup	1¼ cups
vegetable oil	2 tbs.	3 tbs.	4 tbs.
honey	2 tbs.	3 tbs.	4 tbs.
salt	½ tsp.	¾ tsp.	1 tsp.
barley flour	¼ cup	⅓ cup	½ cup
whole wheat flour	¼ cup	⅓ cup	½ cup
white bread flour	2 cups	2⅔ cups	3¼ cups
yeast	1 tsp.	1½ tsp.	2 tsp.
water or flour	1 tablespoon at a time if and as needed to obtain a smooth dough ball		

RECOMMENDED CYCLE   basic white

POTATO SOURDOUGH

The (instant) potato flakes give this a nice potato flavor without the hassle of cooking potatoes!

	1 lb.	**1½ lb.**	**2 lb.**
water	⅓ cup	½ cup	½ cup
sourdough culture	⅔ cup	¾ cup	1 cup
butter or margarine	1 tbs.	1½ tbs.	2 tbs.
sugar	1 tbs.	1½ tbs.	1½ tbs.
potato flakes	¼ cup	⅓ cup	½ cup
salt	½ tsp.	¾ tsp.	1 tsp.
white bread flour	2 cups	3 cups	3½ cups
yeast	1 tsp.	1½ tsp.	2 tsp.
water or flour	1 tablespoon at a time if and as needed to obtain a smooth dough ball		

RECOMMENDED CYCLE　　　basic white, French

ANADAMA SOURDOUGH

Anadama is traditionally made with cornmeal and molasses — this is a sourdough version which you'll like.

	1 lb.	1½ lb.	2 lb.
water	⅓ cup	½ cup	⅔ cup
sourdough culture	⅔ cup	¾ cup	1 cup
vegetable oil	1 tbs.	1½ tbs.	2 tbs.
molasses	2 tbs.	3 tbs.	¼ cup
salt	½ tsp.	¾ tsp.	1 tsp.
cornmeal	½ cup	⅔ cup	¾ cup
white bread flour	2 cups	3 cups	3½ cups
vital gluten	1 tbs.	1½ tbs.	2 tbs.
yeast	1 tsp.	1½ tsp.	2 tsp.
water or flour	1 tablespoon at a time if and as needed to obtain a smooth dough ball		

RECOMMENDED CYCLE   basic white, French

HONEY KAMUT SOURDOUGH

Honey was so highly valued in ancient Egypt that it was used as a tribute or payment and as food for sacred animals! Kamut is said to have originated in Egypt. This bread combines the two for a nutritious, flavorful bread.

	1 lb.	1½ lb.	2 lb.
water	½ cup	⅔ cup	¾ cup
sourdough culture	⅔ cup	¾ cup	1 cup
vegetable oil	1 tbs.	1½ tbs.	2 tbs.
honey	2 tbs.	3 tbs.	¼ cup
salt	½ tsp.	¾ tsp.	1 tsp.
kamut flour	½ cup	⅔ cup	¾ cup
white bread flour	2 cups	3 cups	3½ cups
yeast	1 tsp.	1½ tsp.	2 tsp.
water or flour	1 tablespoon at a time if and as needed to obtain a smooth dough ball		

RECOMMENDED CYCLE   sweet, basic white, French

NEW ENGLAND PIONEER BREAD

The New England pioneers combined their sourdough cultures with ingredients found locally to develop new recipes. This is one recipe which they may have enjoyed using locally grown corn and maple syrup. The vital gluten is optional for a lighter textured loaf.

	1 lb.	**1½ lb.**	**2 lb.**
water	⅓ cup	½ cup	⅔ cup
sourdough culture	⅔ cup	¾ cup	1 cup
vegetable oil	1 tbs.	1½ tbs.	2 tbs.
maple syrup	2 tbs.	3 tbs.	¼ cup
salt	½ tsp.	¾ tsp.	1 tsp.
cornmeal	¼ cup	⅓ cup	½ cup
white bread flour	2 cups	3 cups	3½ cups
vital gluten, optional	1½ tsp.	2 tsp.	1 tbs.
yeast	1 tsp.	1½ tsp.	2 tsp.
water or flour	1 tablespoon at a time if and as needed to obtain a smooth dough ball		

RECOMMENDED CYCLE   sweet, basic white, French

RYE SOURDOUGH

Rye flour and sourdough just seem to go hand and hand! The vital gluten is not necessary but it will give you a higher rising, lighter textured loaf.

	1 lb.	1½ lb.	2 lb.
water	⅓ cup	½ cup	⅔ cup
sourdough culture	⅔ cup	¾ cup	1 cup
vegetable oil	1 tbs.	1½ tbs.	2 tbs.
molasses	1 tbs.	1½ tbs.	2 tbs.
caraway seeds, optional	2 tsp.	1 tbs.	1⅓ tbs.
salt	½ tsp.	¾ tsp.	1 tsp.
sugar	1 tbs.	1½ tbs.	2 tbs.
rye flour	¾ cup	1 cup	1⅛ cups
white bread flour	1½ cups	2¼ cups	3 cups
vital gluten	1 tbs.	1½ tbs.	2 tbs.
yeast	1 tsp.	1½ tsp.	2 tsp.
water or flour	1 tablespoon at a time if and as needed to obtain a smooth dough ball		

RECOMMENDED CYCLE   basic white, whole wheat

MULTI-GRAIN SOURDOUGH

Multi-grain cereal blends (7, 9 or 12 grain) may be found in some large grocery stores or in health food stores. A typical blend consists of cracked wheat, barley, corn, millet, oats, triticale, rice and a variety of seeds.

	1 lb.	**1½ lb.**	**2 lb.**
water	½ cup	⅔ cup	¾ cup
sourdough culture	⅔ cup	¾ cup	1 cup
butter or margarine	1 tbs.	1½ tbs.	2 tbs.
brown sugar	2 tbs.	2½ tbs.	3 tbs.
salt	½ tsp.	¾ tsp.	1 tsp.
7 or 9 grain cereal	½ cup	⅔ cup	¾ cup
white bread flour	2 cups	3 cups	3½ cups
vital gluten	1 tbs.	1 tbs.	1½ tbs.
yeast	1 tsp.	1½ tsp.	2 tsp.
water or flour	1 tablespoon at a time if and as needed to obtain a smooth dough ball		

RECOMMENDED CYCLE sweet, basic white, whole wheat, French

CRACKED WHEAT SOURDOUGH

Measure the water and the cracked wheat into the pan and soak for 30 to 40 minutes. Then add all remaining ingredients and start the machine. If you have a Welbilt or DAK machine, you should soak the cracked wheat in a separate bowl to avoid water leaking into the machine. Be careful to adjust water or flour to correct consistency.

	1 lb.	**1½ lb.**	**2 lb.**
water	½ cup	⅔ cup	¾ cup
cracked wheat	½ cup	⅔ cup	¾ cup
sourdough culture	⅔ cup	¾ cup	1 cup
vegetable oil	1 tbs.	1½ tbs.	2 tbs.
honey	2 tbs.	3 tbs.	¼ cup
salt	½ tsp.	¾ tsp.	1 tsp.
white bread flour	2 cups	3 cups	3½ cups
vital gluten	1 tbs.	1½ tbs.	2 tbs.
yeast	1 tsp.	1½ tsp.	2 tsp.
water or flour	1 tablespoon at a time if and as needed to obtain a smooth dough ball		

RECOMMENDED CYCLE   sweet, basic white, whole wheat

BRAN SOURDOUGH

Both bran and germ cut the elastic network made by the gluten in the flour. This means that this bread is low rising and dense. Adding the vital wheat gluten will help.

	1 lb.	1½ lb.	2 lb.
water	¼ cup	⅓ cup	½ cup
sourdough culture	⅔ cup	¾ cup	1 cup
vegetable oil	1 tbs.	1½ tbs.	2 tbs.
honey or maple syrup	2 tbs.	2½ tbs.	3 tbs.
salt	½ tsp.	¾ tsp.	1 tsp.
wheat germ	2 tbs.	3 tbs.	¼ cup
wheat or oat bran	¼ cup	⅓ cup	½ cup
whole wheat flour	¼ cup	⅓ cup	½ cup
white bread flour	1½ cups	2⅓ cups	3 cups
vital gluten	2 tsp.	1 tbs.	1½ tbs.
yeast	1 tsp.	1½ tsp.	2 tsp.
water or flour	1 tablespoon at a time if and as needed to obtain a smooth dough ball		

RECOMMENDED CYCLE   sweet, basic white, whole wheat

SEEDED SOURDOUGH

The seeds add lots of flavor and crunch.

	1 lb.	**1½ lb.**	**2 lb.**
water	¼ cup	⅓ cup	½ cup
sourdough culture	⅔ cup	¾ cup	1 cup
vegetable oil	1 tbs.	1½ tbs.	2 tbs.
honey or maple syrup	1 tbs.	1½ tbs.	2 tbs.
salt	½ tsp.	¾ tsp.	1 tsp.
poppy seeds	1 tbs.	1½ tbs.	2 tbs.
sesame seeds	1 tbs.	1½ tbs.	2 tbs.
white bread flour	2 cups	3 cups	3½ cups
yeast	1 tsp.	1½ tsp.	2 tsp.
water or flour	1 tablespoon at a time if and as needed to obtain a smooth dough ball		
*sunflower kernels	¼ cup	⅓ cup	½ cup

RECOMMENDED CYCLE   raisin, sweet, basic white

*Add sunflower kernels at the beep or appropriate time for your machine.

GARLIC BASIL SOURDOUGH

If using fresh, chopped basil, triple the amount given. This is a superb accompaniment to a tomato based meal. If there is any left, it makes good croutons. Some people say that bread recipes using fresh garlic do not rise well for them — we don't have that problem in the test kitchen.

	1 lb.	**1½ lb.**	**2 lb.**
water	⅓ cup	½ cup	⅔ cup
sourdough culture	⅔ cup	¾ cup	1 cup
minced garlic	1 tsp.	1½ tsp.	2 tsp.
margarine or butter	1 tbs.	1½ tbs.	2 tbs.
sugar	1 tbs.	1½ tbs.	2 tbs.
salt	½ tsp.	¾ tsp.	1 tsp.
dried basil	1½ tsp.	2 tsp.	1 tbs.
white bread flour	2 cups	3 cups	3½ cups
yeast	1 tsp.	1½ tsp.	2 tsp.
water or flour	1 tablespoon at a time if and as needed to obtain a smooth dough ball		

RECOMMENDED CYCLE   basic white, French

CINNAMON RAISIN NUT BREAD

At first glance, you may think that a sweet bread such as cinnamon raisin would not blend with a sourdough, but it does quite well. Adjust cinnamon to taste if desired.

	1 lb.	1½ lb.	2 lb.
water	⅓ cup	½ cup	⅔ cup
sourdough culture	⅔ cup	¾ cup	1 cup
margarine or butter	1 tbs.	1½ tbs.	2 tbs.
sugar	1 tbs.	1½ tbs.	2 tbs.
cinnamon	1 tsp.	1½ tsp.	2 tsp.
salt	½ tsp.	¾ tsp.	1 tsp.
white bread flour	2 cups	3 cups	3½ cups
yeast	1 tsp.	1½ tsp.	2 tsp.
water or flour	1 tablespoon at a time if and as needed to obtain a smooth dough ball		
*raisins	⅓ cup	½ cup	½ cup
*chopped walnuts	¼ cup	⅓ cup	½ cup

RECOMMENDED CYCLE   sweet, raisin or white

*add raisins and nuts at the beep or appropriate time for your machine

SESAME ANISE BREAD

Sesame and anise seeds are common in both Mexican and Middle Eastern cooking. Somehow, the flavor just seems to blend perfectly with sourdough.

	1 lb.	1½ lb.	2 lb.
water	⅓ cup	½ cup	⅔ cup
sourdough culture	⅔ cup	¾ cup	1 cup
olive oil	1 tbs.	1½ tbs.	2 tbs.
honey	1 tbs.	1½ tbs.	2 tbs.
salt	½ tsp.	¾ tsp.	1 tsp.
anise seeds	1 tbs.	1½ tbs.	2 tbs.
sesame seeds	2 tbs.	3 tbs.	¼ cup
white bread flour	2 cups	3 cups	3½ cups
yeast	1 tsp.	1½ tsp.	2 tsp.
water or flour	1 tablespoon at a time if and as needed to obtain a smooth dough ball		

RECOMMENDED CYCLE   basic white, French

APRICOT ALMOND BREAD

Both the apricots and almonds blend beautifully with a sourdough flavor in this bread. Serve as a breakfast toast or as a sandwich bread with poultry.

	1 lb.	**1½ lb.**	**2 lb.**
water	⅓ cup	½ cup	⅔ cup
sourdough culture	⅔ cup	¾ cup	1 cup
margarine or butter	1 tbs.	1½ tbs.	2 tbs.
sugar	2 tbs.	3 tbs.	¼ cup
orange peel	½ tsp.	¾ tsp.	1 tsp.
salt	½ tsp.	¾ tsp.	1 tsp.
white bread flour	2 cups	3 cups	3½ cups
yeast	1 tsp.	1½ tsp.	2 tsp.
water or flour	1 tablespoon at a time if and as needed to obtain a smooth dough ball		
*diced dried apricots	⅓ cup	½ cup	⅔ cup
*slivered almonds	⅓ cup	½ cup	⅔ cup

RECOMMENDED CYCLE sweet, raisin or white

*add at the beep or appropriate time for your machine

FIG SOURDOUGH

Use dried figs for this flavorful bread. This bread may be made as is, or add the ingredients for one of the variations. All three loaves are sure to please!

	1 lb.	1½ lb.	2 lb.
water	¼ cup	⅓ cup	½ cup
sourdough culture	⅔ cup	¾ cup	1 cup
margarine or butter	1 tbs.	1½ tbs.	2 tbs.
sugar	2 tbs.	3 tbs.	¼ cup
orange peel	½ tsp.	¾ tsp.	1 tsp.
salt	½ tsp.	¾ tsp.	1 tsp.
white bread flour	2 cups	3 cups	3½ cups
yeast	1 tsp.	1½ tsp.	2 tsp.
water or flour	1 tablespoon at a time if and as needed to obtain a smooth dough ball		
*diced dried figs	⅓ cup	½ cup	⅔ cup
RECOMMENDED CYCLE	sweet, raisin or white		

*add at the beep or appropriate time for your machine

VARIATION I: ORANGE FIG

Add these ingredients in addition to the basic recipe on page 152.

dried orange peel	1 tsp.	1½ tsp.	2 tsp.
vanilla extract	1 tsp.	1½ tsp.	2 tsp.

VARIATION II: ANISE FIG

Omit the orange peel in the basic recipe on page 152 and add this ingredient.

anise seeds	1½ tsp.	2 tsp.	1 tbs.

ALMOND DATE SOURDOUGH

This bread may be made as is, or add the ingredients for one of the variations. Pine nuts may be substituted for the almonds in the variations.

	1 lb.	1½ lb.	2 lb.
water	¼ cup	⅓ cup	½ cup
sourdough culture	⅔ cup	¾ cup	1 cup
olive oil	1 tbs.	1½ tbs.	2 tbs.
honey	2 tbs.	3 tbs.	¼ cup
salt	½ tsp.	¾ tsp.	1 tsp.
white bread flour	2 cups	3 cups	3½ cups
yeast	1 tsp.	1½ tsp.	2 tsp.
water or flour	1 tablespoon at a time if and as needed to obtain a smooth dough ball		
*diced dried dates	⅓ cup	½ cup	⅔ cup
*slivered almonds	⅓ cup	½ cup	⅔ cup

RECOMMENDED CYCLE   sweet, raisin or white

*add at the beep or appropriate time for your machine

VARIATION I: LEMON ALMOND DATE

Add this ingredient to the basic recipe on page 154.

dried lemon peel	1 tsp.	1½ tsp.	2 tsp.

VARIATION II: FLAVORED ALMOND DATE

Add these ingredients to the basic recipe on page 154.

ground coriander	¼ tsp.	⅓ tsp.	½ tsp.
ground cumin	¼ tsp.	⅓ tsp.	½ tsp.
ground cinnamon	¼ tsp.	⅓ tsp.	½ tsp.

WALNUT RYE

This nutty-flavored rye rises moderately well and has a nice, dense texture. If you want a higher rise with a lighter texture, add a tablespoon or two of vital gluten.

	1 lb.	1½ lb.	2 lb.
water	⅓ cup	½ cup	⅔ cup
sourdough culture	¾ cup	1 cup	1¼ cups
walnut oil or vegetable oil	1 tbs.	1½ tbs.	2 tbs.
sugar	2 tbs.	3 tbs.	¼ cup
salt	½ tsp.	¾ tsp.	1 tsp.
rye flour	¼ cup	⅓ cup	½ cup
whole wheat flour	¼ cup	⅓ cup	½ cup
white bread flour	2 cups	2⅔ cups	3 cups
yeast	1 tsp.	1½ tsp.	2 tsp.
water or flour	1 tablespoon at a time if and as needed to obtain a smooth dough ball		
*chopped walnuts	⅓ cup	½ cup	⅔ cup

RECOMMENDED CYCLE   basic white

*add at the beep or appropriate time for your machine

CORN RYE

A light version of a Jewish corn rye. The caraway seeds may be adjusted to taste if desired.

	1 lb.	**1½ lb.**	**2 lb.**
water	⅓ cup	½ cup	⅔ cup
sourdough culture	¾ cup	1 cup	1¼ cups
butter or margarine	1 tbs.	1½ tbs.	2 tbs.
sugar	2 tbs.	3 tbs.	4 tbs.
salt	½ tsp.	¾ tsp.	1 tsp.
caraway seeds	1 tsp.	1½ tsp.	2 tsp.
cornmeal	⅓ cup	½ cup	⅔ cup
rye flour	⅓ cup	½ cup	⅔ cup
white bread flour	1½ cups	2⅓ cups	3 cups
vital wheat gluten	1 tbs.	1½ tbs.	2 tbs.
yeast	1 tsp.	1½ tsp.	2 tsp.
water or flour	1 tablespoon at a time if and as needed to obtain a smooth dough ball		

RECOMMENDED CYCLE   wheat, sweet, basic white, French

GERMAN FARM BREAD

This is traditionally made in a round shape but it tastes just as great in the machine pan shape! This rises nicely.

	1 lb.	**1½ lb.**	**2 lb.**
water	½ cup	⅔ cup	¾ cup
sourdough culture	¾ cup	1 cup	1¼ cups
butter or margarine	1 tbs.	1½ tbs.	2 tbs.
brown sugar	2 tbs.	3 tbs.	¼ cup
salt	½ tsp.	¾ tsp.	1 tsp.
oats	⅓ cup	½ cup	⅔ cup
whole wheat flour	⅓ cup	½ cup	⅔ cup
white bread flour	1½ cups	2⅓ cups	3 cups
vital gluten	1 tbs.	1½ tbs.	2 tbs.
yeast	1 tsp.	1½ tsp.	2 tsp.
water or flour	1 tablespoon at a time if and as needed to obtain a smooth dough ball		

RECOMMENDED CYCLE   sweet, basic white, whole wheat

BLACK FOREST SOURDOUGH

The onion can affect the moisture of the dough — watch it carefully.

	1 lb.	**1½ lb.**	**2 lb.**
water	¼ cup	⅓ cup	½ cup
sourdough culture	¾ cup	1 cup	1¼ cups
diced onion	2 tbs.	3 tbs.	¼ cup
butter or margarine	1 tbs.	1½ tbs.	2 tbs.
brown sugar	2 tbs.	3 tbs.	¼ cup
mustard seeds	1 tsp.	1½ tsp.	2 tsp.
or ground mustard	⅓ tsp.	½ tsp.	⅔ tsp.
caraway seeds	1 tsp.	1½ tsp.	2 tsp.
salt	½ tsp.	¾ tsp.	1 tsp.
rye flour	½ cup	⅔ cup	¾ cup
white bread flour	2 cups	3 cups	3½ cups
vital gluten, optional	1 tbs.	1½ tbs.	2 tbs.
yeast	1 tsp.	1½ tsp.	2 tsp.
water or flour	1 tablespoon at a time if and as needed to obtain a smooth dough ball		

RECOMMENDED CYCLE   sweet, basic white, whole wheat

NEW WORLD GRAIN BREAD

Both quinoa and amaranth are grains which are native to the Americas and have recently been revived due to their high nutritional value. The grains themselves are only the size of poppy or sesame seeds and are added directly to this bread. Try toasting this bread for an exciting treat as the grains may "pop!"

	1 lb.	**1½ lb.**	**2 lb.**
water	⅓ cup	½ cup	⅔ cup
sourdough culture	⅔ cup	¾ cup	1 cup
margarine or butter	1 tbs.	1½ tbs.	2 tbs.
brown sugar	1 tbs.	1½ tbs.	2 tbs.
salt	½ tsp.	¾ tsp.	1 tsp.
quinoa grains	2 tbs.	3 tbs.	¼ cup
amaranth grains	2 tbs.	3 tbs.	¼ cup
white bread flour	2 cups	3 cups	3½ cups
yeast	1 tsp.	1½ tsp.	2 tsp.
water or flour	1 tablespoon at a time if and as needed to obtain a smooth dough ball		

RECOMMENDED CYCLE   basic white, whole wheat, French

ONION CHEESE SOURDOUGH

The culture, the cheese and the scallions all have varying moisture content, so check the dough after 5 minutes of kneading and adjust if necessary. The cheese and scallions may be added at the beginning, but it is best to add them at the raisin beep or appropriate time for your machine. Use cheddar or spicy Monterey Jack cheese.

	1 lb.	**1½ lb.**	**2 lb.**
water	⅓ cup	½ cup	½ cup
sourdough culture	⅔ cup	¾ cup	1 cup
margarine or butter	1 tbs.	1½ tbs.	2 tbs.
sugar	1 tbs.	1½ tbs.	2 tbs.
salt	½ tsp.	¾ tsp.	1 tsp.
white bread flour	2¼ cups	3 cups	3½ cups
yeast	1 tsp.	1½ tsp.	2 tsp.
water or flour	1 tablespoon at a time if and as needed to obtain a smooth dough ball		
*grated cheese	⅓ cup	½ cup	⅔ cup
*scallion, diced (white and green)	1	1½	2

RECOMMENDED CYCLE sweet, basic white

DRIED TOMATO BASIL BREAD

Use home-dried or commercially prepared sun-dried tomatoes for this bread. Cut the tomatoes into small pieces and soak them in the water and olive oil for 5 minutes before adding the remaining ingredients. This may be done right in the bread machine pan unless you have a DAK, Welbilt or Decosonic, in which case they must be soaked in the liquid measuring cup.

	1 lb.	1½ lb.	2 lb.
water	¼ cup	⅓ cup	½ cup
sourdough culture	⅔ cup	¾ cup	1 cup
olive oil	1 tbs.	1½ tbs.	2 tbs.
sun-dried tomatoes	2 tbs.	3 tbs.	¼ cup
sugar	1½ tsp.	2 tsp.	1 tbs.
salt	½ tsp.	¾ tsp.	1 tsp.
dried basil	1½ tsp.	2 tsp.	1 tbs.
white bread flour	2 cups	3 cups	3½ cups
yeast	1 tsp.	1½ tsp.	2 tsp.
water or flour	1 tablespoon at a time if and as needed to obtain a smooth dough ball		

RECOMMENDED CYCLE   basic white, French

VARIATION: DRIED TOMATO GARLIC

Add ingredient to the basic recipe on page 162.

| minced garlic | 1 tsp. | 1½ tsp. | 2 tsp. |

ORANGE CRAISIN BREAD

Craisins are dried, sweetened cranberries which may be found in gourmet food stores or in some large grocery stores. Orange juice concentrate may be used in place of the vegetable oil for a stronger orange flavor — and no fat.

	1 lb.	1½ lb.	2 lb.
water	⅓ cup	½ cup	⅔ cup
sourdough culture	⅔ cup	¾ cup	1 cup
vegetable oil	1 tbs.	1½ tbs.	2 tbs.
honey	1 tbs.	1½ tbs.	2 tbs.
orange peel	1 tbs.	1½ tbs.	2 tbs.
salt	½ tsp.	¾ tsp.	1 tsp.
white bread flour	2 cups	3 cups	3½ cups
yeast	1 tsp.	1½ tsp.	2 tsp.
water or flour	1 tablespoon at a time if and as needed to obtain a smooth dough ball		
*craisins	⅓ cup	½ cup	⅔ cup

RECOMMENDED CYCLE   sweet, raisin or white

*add craisins at the beep or appropriate time for your machine

IRISH SOURDOUGH

This is a cross between an Irish soda bread which is traditionally made with buttermilk and a sourdough bread. A winner!

	1 lb.	1½ lb.	2 lb.
water	½ cup	⅔ cup	¾ cup
sourdough culture	⅔ cup	¾ cup	1 cup
margarine or butter	1 tbs.	1½ tbs.	2 tbs.
sugar	1 tbs.	1½ tbs.	2 tbs.
caraway seeds	1 tbs.	1½ tbs.	2 tbs.
salt	½ tsp.	¾ tsp.	1 tsp.
white bread flour	2½ cups	3 cups	3½ cups
yeast	1 tsp.	1½ tsp.	2 tsp.
water or flour	1 tablespoon at a time if and as needed to obtain a smooth dough ball		
*raisins	½ cup	⅔ cup	¾ cup

RECOMMENDED CYCLE   sweet, raisin or white

*add raisins at the beep or appropriate time for your machine

SOURCES

To obtain a free brochure on sourdough cultures from Ed Wood, write to:
Sourdoughs International, Inc.
P.O. Box 993
Cascade, ID 83611

Call for a free catalog or ordering information:

Arrowhead Mills, Inc. (806) 364-0730 (grains and flours)

Cal Gar Goldrush Sourdough (201) 691-2928 (San Francisco style sourdough starter)

Garden Spot Distributors (800) 829-5100 (grains, flours, cereals)

Great Valley Mills (800) 688-6455 (stone ground flours)

Jaffee Bros. Inc. (619) 749-1133 (grains, flours and other food items)

King Arthur Flour (800) 827-6836 (flours, grains, sourdough starters, other items)

K-Tec (800) 288-6455 (grain mills, grains, cereals, other bread baking items)

Montana Flour and Grains (406) 622-5436 (kamut flour)

Purity Foods (517) 351-9231 (spelt flour)

Walnut Acres (800) 433-3998 (organic farm: flours, grains, etc.)

INDEX

SERVE CREATIVE, EASY, NUTRITIOUS MEALS WITH NITTY GRITTY® COOKBOOKS

Extra-Special Crockery Pot Recipes
Clay Cookery
Marinades
Deep-Fried Indulgences
Cooking with Parchment Paper
The Garlic Cookbook
Flatbreads From Around the World
From Your Ice Cream Maker
Favorite Cookie Recipes
Cappuccino/Espresso: The Book of Beverages
Indoor Grilling
Slow Cooking
The Best Pizza is Made at Home
The Well Dressed Potato
Convection Oven Cookery
The Steamer Cookbook
The Pasta Machine Cookbook
The Versatile Rice Cooker

The Dehydrator Cookbook
The Bread Machine Cookbook
The Bread Machine Cookbook II
The Bread Machine Cookbook III
The Bread Machine Cookbook IV
The Bread Machine Cookbook V
Worldwide Sourdoughs From Your Bread Machine
Recipes for the Pressure Cooker
The New Blender Book
The Sandwich Maker Cookbook
Waffles
The Coffee Book
The Juicer Book
The Juicer Book II
Bread Baking (traditional), revised
No Salt, No Sugar, No Fat Cookbook

Cooking for 1 or 2
Quick and Easy Pasta Recipes
The 9x13 Pan Cookbook
Chocolate Cherry Tortes and Other Lowfat Delights
Low Fat American Favorites
Now That's Italian!
Fabulous Fiber Cookery
Low Salt, Low Sugar, Low Fat Desserts
Healthy Cooking on the Run
Healthy Snacks for Kids
Muffins, Nut Breads and More
The Wok
New Ways to Enjoy Chicken
Favorite Seafood Recipes
New International Fondue Cookbook

Write or call for our free catalog.
BRISTOL PUBLISHING ENTERPRISES, INC.
P.O. Box 1737, San Leandro, CA 94577
(800) 346-4889; in California (510) 895-4461